100% NEW

DEVELOPING MATHEMATICS

**Customisable
teaching resources
for mathematics**

UNDERSTANDING SHAPES AND MEASURES

Ages 7–8

Hilary Koll and
Steve Mills

D1147168

A & C Black • London

Contents

Relate 2-D shapes and 3-D solids to drawings of them; describe, visualise, classify, draw and make the shapes

Draw and complete shapes with reflective symmetry; draw the reflection of a shape in a mirror line along one side

Read and record the vocabulary of position, direction and movement, using the four compass directions to describe movement about a grid

Use a set-square to draw right angles and to identify right angles in 2-D shapes; compare angles with a right angle; recognise that a straight line is equivalent to two right angles

Know the relationships between kilometres and metres, metres and centimetres, kilograms and grams, litres and millilitres

CR
516.
15
JND

Published 2008 by A & C Black Publishers Limited
36 Soho Square, London W1D 3QY
www.acblack.com

ISBN 978-1-4081-0057-8

Copyright text © Hilary Koll and Steve Mills 2008
Copyright illustrations © Mike Brownlow 2008
Copyright cover illustration © Jan McCafferty 2008
Editors: Lynne Williamson and Marie Lister
Designed by Billin Design Solutions Ltd

The author and publishers would like to thank Catherine Yemm
and Judith Wells for their advice in producing this series of books.

A CIP catalogue record for this book is available from the
British Library.

Printed and bound in Great Britain by Halstan Printing Group,
Amersham, Buckinghamshire.

A & C Black uses paper produced with elemental chlorine-free
pulp, harvested from managed sustainable forests.

Introduction

100% New Developing Mathematics: Understanding Shapes and Measures is a series of seven photocopiable activity books for children aged 4 to 11, designed to be used during the daily maths lesson. The books focus on the skills and concepts for Understanding Shape and Measuring as outlined in the National Strategy's *Primary Framework for literacy and mathematics*. The activities are intended to be used in the time allocated to pupil activities; they aim to reinforce the knowledge and develop the facts, skills and understanding explored during the main part of the lesson, and to provide practice and consolidation of the objectives contained in the Framework document.

Understanding shape

This strand of the *Primary Framework for mathematics* is concerned with helping pupils to develop awareness and understanding of the properties of shapes, spatial concepts, and ideas of position and location. It covers the properties of 2-D and 3-D shapes, including angles and symmetries, together with ways of describing positions in grids, such as using coordinates.

Measuring

The 'Measuring' strand, which is also addressed in this book, includes the main measurement topics such as length, mass and capacity, together with ideas of time, area and perimeter. These topics cover estimating, comparing and measuring, including using standard metric units and converting between them.

Understanding Shapes and Measures Ages 7-8

supports the teaching of mathematics by providing a series of activities to develop spatial vocabulary in order to increase awareness of properties of shape and measurement concepts. The following learning objectives are covered:

- relate 2-D shapes and 3-D solids to drawings of them; describe, visualise, classify, draw and make the shapes;

- draw and complete shapes with reflective symmetry; draw the reflection of a shape in a mirror line along one side;

- read and record the vocabulary of position, direction and movement, using the four compass directions to describe movement about a grid;

- use a set-square to draw right angles and to identify right angles in 2-D shapes; compare angles with a right angle; recognise that a straight line is equivalent to two right angles;

- know the relationships between kilometres and metres, metres and centimetres, kilograms and grams, litres and millilitres;

- choose and use appropriate units to estimate, measure and record measurements.

- read, to the nearest division and half-division, scales that are numbered or partially numbered; use the information to measure and draw to a suitable degree of accuracy;

- read the time on a 12-hour digital clock and to the nearest 5 minutes on an analogue clock;

- calculate time intervals and find start or end times for a given time interval.

Extension

Many of the activity sheets end with a challenge (**Now try this!**) which reinforces and extends children's learning, and provides the teacher with an opportunity for assessment. These might include harder questions, with numbers from a higher range, than those in the main part of the activity sheet. Some challenges are open-ended questions and provide opportunity for children to think mathematically for themselves. Occasionally the challenge will require additional paper or that the children write on the reverse of the sheet itself. Many of the activities encourage children to generate their own questions or puzzles for a partner to solve.

Organisation

Very little equipment is needed, but it will be useful to have available: rulers, scissors, coloured pencils, dice, counters, glue or transparent tape, string, interlocking cubes, solid shapes and small mirrors. You also need to provide matchsticks for page 14 and clocks with movable, geared hands for pages 58–62.

The children should also have access to measuring equipment to give them practical experience of length, mass and capacity.

Where possible, children's work should be supported by ICT equipment, such as number lines and tracks on interactive whiteboards, or computer software for comparing numbers and measures. It is also vital that children's experiences are introduced in real-life contexts and through practical activities. The teachers' notes at the foot of each page and the more detailed notes on pages 6 to 11 suggest ways in which this can be done effectively.

To help teachers select appropriate learning experiences for the children, the activities are grouped into sections within the book. However, the activities are not expected to be used in this order unless stated otherwise. The sheets are intended to support, rather than direct, the teacher's planning.

Some activities can be made easier or more challenging by masking or substituting numbers. You may wish to re-use pages by copying them onto card and laminating them.

Accompanying CD

The enclosed CD-ROM contains all of the activity sheets from the book as PDF and Word files so you can edit them for printing or saving. This means that modifications can be made to further differentiate the activities to suit individual pupils' needs.

Teachers' notes

Brief notes are provided at the foot of each page, giving ideas and suggestions for maximising the effectiveness of the activity sheets. These can be masked before copying.

Further explanations of the activities can be found on pages 6 to 11, together with examples of questions you can ask.

Whole class warm-up activities

The tools provided in A & C Black's Maths Skills and Practice CD-ROMs can be used as introductory activities for use with the whole class. In the Maths Skills and Practice CD-ROM 3 (ISBN 9780713673197) the following activities and games could be used to introduce or reinforce 'Shapes and Measures' objectives:

- Basket ball
- 3-D
- Time quiz
- Position words

The following activities provide some practical ideas which can be used to introduce or reinforce the main teaching part of the lesson, or to provide an interesting basis for discussion.

Understanding shape

Twenty questions

Hide a 3-D shape in a bag and ask the children to find out which shape it is by asking questions. You can only answer 'yes' or 'no' to their questions. Challenge the children to guess the shape in twenty questions.

Great grid

Display a grid on the board like the one shown. Tell the children to imagine a counter on a square, such as D3, and to describe how the counter is to be moved, for example:
2 squares East. Ask the children to give the new position of the counter. Instructions can be made more complicated
by giving several steps, for example: 2 squares East and 3 squares North.

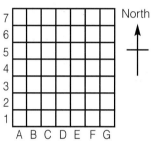

Measuring
Make a metre

Call out lengths in centimetres that are less than a metre, for example 50 cm, 70 cm, 22 cm, and ask the children to give the length that would make this measurement up to 1 metre: 50 cm, 30 cm, 78 cm. Hold up a metre stick and show the lengths to help the children to visualise the measurements. The same activity can be adapted for kilograms or litres, where measurements such as 350 g or 900 ml are given.

Time moves on

In the same way that children sitting in a circle might say numbers in a sequence, for example 2, 4, 6, 8, begin by saying a time such as '4 o'clock'. Moving around the circle, ask the children to say the time that is an hour later or earlier, for example: 4 o'clock, 5 o'clock, 6 o'clock, 7 o'clock... Once children understand the idea, time sequences that involve counting on or back in steps of half an hour, a quarter of an hour, or in 10- or 5-minute intervals can be continued, for example: Twenty past 11, half past 11, twenty to 12, ten to 12... Hold up a clock to show the times and discuss different ways of saying the same time, for example 'twenty to 12' or '11:40'.

Notes on the activities

Understanding shape

Relate 2-D shapes and 3-D solids to drawings of them; describe, visualise, classify, draw and make the shapes

It is vital that children are given extensive opportunity to work practically with shapes, construction materials, boxes, containers, sand, water and so on, in order to develop a broad understanding of the nature and properties of 2-D and 3-D shapes. The following activities can supplement these practical tasks and provide contexts and stimuli that can be more fully explored in the classroom. Encourage the children to develop vocabulary skills by ensuring that activities are undertaken in pairs or small groups and that whole class discussions take place frequently. The activities below can be used to encourage children to develop language skills and to develop awareness of the properties of shapes.

Children should be introduced to faces, vertices and edges of 3-D shapes and should become familiar with reflective symmetries of 2-D shapes. An awareness of right angles in shapes should also be developed.

Spot the difference (page 13)

It is important that children begin to appreciate when two shapes have similarities and differences. The pairs of shapes on this worksheet are different because they have been enlarged (or reduced), reflected, stretched, or because one vertex has been moved. The children should be encouraged to develop the necessary vocabulary to describe such features and to identify aspects that have remained the same. Pairs could make jottings on the backs of the cards as a reminder for when whole-class discussion takes place.

SUGGESTED QUESTIONS:

- How many sides/corners/angles does this shape have?
- Are the sides/corners/angles of this shape the same or different?

A sticky situation (page 14)

It is not expected that children will be able to name the four-sided shapes as a rhombus or a trapezium at this stage, but they should be learning that it is possible to make four-sided shapes other than rectangles or squares, and that all are known as quadrilaterals. Note that there are many different answers to this investigation, depending on the positioning of the sticks.

SUGGESTED PROMPT/QUESTIONS:

- Do you know what this shape is called?
- Describe the shape to me. What does it remind you of?
- How many sides/corners/angles does it have?

Stargazer (page 15)

Encourage the children to realise that there are several possible answers for some of the shapes.

SUGGESTED QUESTIONS:

- How many sides does a pentagon have?
- Is this shape you have drawn symmetrical?
- What do you call a shape with four straight sides?

Draw and name game (page 16)

The children need one worksheet per pair. A third child could act as adjudicator, if desired.

At the start of the lesson, discuss some of the descriptions of the shapes on the worksheet and ask children to come to the front of the class to draw shapes to match. Revise the common shape names, including the term 'quadrilateral'. Encourage the children to use a ruler when drawing 2-D shapes.

SUGGESTED QUESTIONS:

- Do you know the name of this shape?
- How many sides/right angles/lines of symmetry has this shape?

Building work (page 17)

Children often struggle to visualise a 3-D solid from a 2-D drawing. If the children find this activity difficult, colour the cubes on the worksheet and give them corresponding coloured cubes with which to build.

When the children carry out the extension activity, encourage them to pick up the models they have made and twist them around to work out which of the shapes are the same. During the plenary, discuss whether the children think that the shapes are different or the same if they are positioned differently on a table.

SUGGESTED QUESTIONS:

- How many cubes have you used to make this shape?
- Can you colour the picture to match the colour of your cubes?

Traffic lights (page 18)

Revise the terms 'faces' and 'edges' and ensure that the children are familiar with the terms 'vertex' and 'vertices', meaning 'corner' and 'corners'. Provide each child with red, orange and green coloured pencils for this activity.

SUGGESTED QUESTIONS:

- What shapes are the faces of a cube/cuboid/triangular prism?
- Which shapes have one or more curved faces?

Shape all-sorts (page 19)

At the start of the lesson, demonstrate how a Carroll diagram is used to show data, drawing attention to the fact that the headings along the top refer to the whole columns and that the other headings refer to the whole rows.

If possible, display the shape names for the children to refer to when completing this activity.

SUGGESTED QUESTIONS:

- Do you know the name of this shape?
- How many faces/vertices has this shape?
- Are its faces curved or straight?

Taboo or not taboo (page 20)

It is important that children have as much experience of describing 3-D shapes and their properties as possible. By making it 'illegal' to use the shape names, attention is focused on the nature of the properties of the shapes.

SUGGESTED PROMPT/QUESTIONS:

- Look at the solid shapes. Which shapes have only one curved face?
- How many edges has this cylinder?

Draw and complete shapes with reflective symmetry; draw the reflection of a shape in a mirror line along one side

Children should become familiar with reflective symmetries of 2-D shapes. Provide lots of practical opportunities for the children to find the lines of symmetry of 2-D shapes by folding paper and then using mirrors. To investigate symmetrical patterns, the children could first have experience of building these on pegboards or with tiles of coloured paper, checking that their patterns are symmetrical by placing mirrors on the lines of symmetry.

Symmetry Cemetery (page 21)

Watch out for the following errors:

line 1 shape 3 – children often mistake as symmetrical;

line 2 shape 5 – children often miss the line of symmetry, as it is neither vertical nor horizontal;

line 3 shape 3 – children often miss the horizontal line of symmetry.

SUGGESTED QUESTIONS:

- Can you draw some more shapes that have one line of symmetry?
- Is the line of symmetry vertical, horizontal or diagonal?

Shape symmetry (page 22)

At the start of the lesson, demonstrate how to place the mirror along the mirror line and lift and replace the mirror to see the paper underneath. Perspex equipment (such as a MIRA) that allows not only the reflection to be seen but also the drawing on the other side of the line can be a useful resource for those children who struggle with mirrors.

SUGGESTED QUESTION/PROMPT:

- Have you checked your reflection?
- Hold the mirror on the mirror line. Lift the mirror and check your drawing underneath.

Mosaic patterns (page 23)

Encourage the children to use a mirror (or a MIRA) to check for the position of the mirror line in each pattern and then to work out where the tiles need to be shaded. Once the tiles have been shaded the children should hold the mirror along the mirror line and then lift it to check whether their answer underneath is correct.

SUGGESTED QUESTIONS:

- Where do you think the mirror line must be?
- Can you use the mirror to check?

Secret symmetry (page 24)

This activity also addresses the objective 'Describing and locating regions in a grid', where children use letters to describe the column and numbers to describe the row, for example A4 or C2.

SUGGESTED QUESTIONS:

- Is your pattern symmetrical?
- Can you use a mirror to help you check?

Dotty symmetry (page 25)

The shapes can be altered to provide further differentiation.

SUGGESTED QUESTIONS:

- How close to the mirror line is this vertex?
- Is this vertex the same distance from the line?

Read and record the vocabulary of position, direction and movement, using the four compass directions to describe movement about a grid

The children should develop an understanding of a range of positional, direction and distance words, and be able to use them to interpret and give their own instructions. Instructions should contain position (such as locating a square in a grid), direction (such as left and right or using the compass points), and movement, indicating the distance of the movement (for example 3 squares, or 4 units).

Lost! (page 26)

This game is very popular with children and provides practice in using the compass points. Provide each child with a small counter and give the group one copy of the worksheet. If desired, the direction cards and game board could be laminated and made into a more permanent classroom resource.

At the start of the lesson, ask the children to tell you what they know about the points of the compass and what the four directions are. Discuss the compass points shown on the worksheet.

SUGGESTED QUESTION:

- If I move to the right on the board, in which compass direction am I moving?

Dodge the dangers (page 27)

Introduce the children to the notation 'N1' to mean 'move 1 square to the north' etc. or, if preferred, alter the worksheet to read '1 square North'.

SUGGESTED QUESTIONS:

- Can you follow another person's instructions?
- Where would you end up?

Lawnmower man (page 28)

At the start of the lesson, stick a sign saying 'North' on the appropriate wall of the classroom. Ask the children to face North, and then ask them to turn to face different directions. Invite a volunteer to be the 'direction caller'.

SUGGESTED QUESTION:

- Can you describe where the lawnmower man went?

Counter tracker (page 29)

Explain how positions can be found on a grid labelled with numbers and letters, like the grid shown on the worksheet. Draw a cross at C5, then draw an arrow to D5 and ask the children to say which direction they have moved in. Repeat for other positions, and then extend to moving in two directions, for example 3 squares West and 1 square South.

SUGGESTED QUESTIONS:

- Can you follow this set of instructions?
- Where would you end up?

Map work (page 30)

Encourage the children to measure the distances as accurately as they can. Most children will be able to measure to the nearest half-centimetre.

SUGGESTED QUESTIONS:

- In which direction from the mosque is the café?
- In which direction from the hotel is the hospital?
- How far away is it?

Use a set-square to draw right angles and to identify right angles in 2-D shapes; compare angles with a right angle; recognise that a straight line is equivalent to two right angles

The basis of all angle work is the idea of turning. Many children have struggled with the ideas of angle because they have been given insufficient time to appreciate turn and have moved too quickly onto static angles, causing misconceptions that the angle between two lines is related to line length, arc length, distance between the two end-points of the lines, and not related to the amount of turn that would take one line onto the other.

Therefore, it is very important that children explore turning practically before they begin to explore angles in static pictures. They should recognise and make whole, half and quarter turns as a precursor for understanding and recognising the nature of right angles.

Learner driver (page 31)

At the start of the lesson, ask the children to tell you everything they know about right angles and to identify examples of right angles in the classroom. Encourage the children to appreciate that right angles do not have to be made from vertical and horizontal lines – they can be diagonally orientated, for example those in the fence in the picture.

SUGGESTED PROMPT/QUESTIONS:

- A right angle is a quarter turn. True or false?
- Is this angle larger or smaller than a right angle?
- How can you check?

It's your turn! (page 32)

At the start of the lesson, ask the children to stand up and face the front of the classroom. Give instructions for turns, for example: 'Turn one right angle anticlockwise'; 'Turn two half turns clockwise'. Encourage the children to turn slowly and not to look at others.

During the plenary, ask the children to explain what they noticed about their answer to question 4. What size turn are two right angles equivalent to?

SUGGESTED PROMPT/QUESTIONS:

- A right angle is a quarter turn. True or false?
- What do you notice about two right angles? Is this the same as a half turn?
- Is a half turn clockwise the same as a half turn anticlockwise?

Learning about turning (page 33)

The answers given on page 64 are those related to the angles up to 180°, i.e. they do not include reflex angles but the closest angle between the two letters (or 180° as in the case of HE). Children who find this work difficult could use a right angle tester (for example the corner of a sheet of paper or the right angle gobbler from page 35) to help them.

SUGGESTED QUESTIONS:

- Is this angle smaller or larger than a right angle?
- Which word involves a turn that is the same as two right angles?

Angle art (page 34)

During the plenary, encourage the children to estimate the size of the smaller angles, for example: 'This looks about half a right angle' or 'This looks about one-third of a right angle'.

SUGGESTED QUESTION:

- Is this angle smaller or larger than a right angle?

Birds' beaks (page 35)

Here, the children must identify the approximate size of an angle in relation to a right angle, for example: 'This looks about half a right angle' or 'This looks about one-third of a right angle'.

They should cut out and use the right angle gobbler to check their estimates.

SUGGESTED QUESTIONS:

- Which of the beaks do you think shows an angle that is about half a right angle?
- Which of the beaks do you think shows an angle that is about one-third of a right angle?
- Which of the beaks do you think shows an angle that is just over a right angle?

Measuring

Know the relationships between kilometres and metres, metres and centimetres, kilograms and grams, litres and millilitres

Children of this age are beginning to become familiar with centimetres, metres, kilometres, grams, kilograms, millilitres and litres. They should know the relationships between the main standard units of length, mass and capacity, and begin to be able to use the units when estimating, measuring, reading and recording measurements.

Stream scheme (page 36)

At the start of the lesson, hold up a metre stick and discuss that there are 100 cm in one metre. Call out some multiples of one hundred as numbers of centimetres and ask the children to say how many metres these would be, showing the lengths both vertically and horizontally.

SUGGESTED QUESTIONS:

- Do you think this is larger or smaller than 1 m?
- Can you show me with your hands how long you think this length is?
- Can you think of something in the room that is about this length?

Ribbons (page 37)

Hold up a two-digit multiple of 10 and ask the children to hold up the complement to 100. Extend to holding up any two-digit number. Discuss the methods that the children used to work out the complements.

SUGGESTED QUESTIONS:

- How many centimetres are there in a metre?
- What method did you use to work out that answer?

How far? (page 38)

This activity could be extended further by finding out how far the children in the class live from the school, and then a related map could be drawn and described.

SUGGESTED QUESTIONS:

- How far away from the school do you think Ella lives?
- Can you draw a house that is about 800 m from the school?

Weight lifters (page 39)

At the start of the lesson, remind the children that 1000 g is the same as 1 kg and pass round weights so that the children can begin to develop a sense of how heavy 1 kg or 1000 g is. Explain that 1 g is the weight of water that would fit into a centimetre cube (if that were possible).

SUGGESTED QUESTION:

- How many grams is the same as 1 kilogram/half a kilogram?

Milkshake mistakes (page 40)

At the start of the lesson, remind the children that 1000 ml is the same as 1 litre and pass round a container, bottle or carton that holds a litre of liquid. This will help the children to begin to develop a sense of how much 1 litre or 1000 ml is. Explain that 1 ml is the amount of water that would fit into a centimetre cube (if that were possible).

SUGGESTED QUESTIONS:

- How did you know that 10 litres is not the same as 1000 ml?
- How did you work out that 3000 ml is the same amount as 3 litres?

Choose and use appropriate units to estimate, measure and record measurements

It is vital that children are given as much practical experience as possible in order that they gain a full appreciation of the units, in particular those of mass and capacity, to enable them to estimate and check that measurements are sensible. Sometimes children learn of the units in an abstract way but are unable to say whether a coin weighs more or less than a gram, or more or less than one kilogram!

Question time (page 41)

These cards could be enlarged and laminated to create a more permanent classroom resource.

SUGGESTED QUESTIONS:

- Which unit do you think would be best?
- Does your partner agree?

Measure master (page 42)

Provide the children with a copy of the worksheet, a dice per pair, and counters in two colours. Show each of the pieces of measuring equipment to the children at the start of the lesson and discuss how they are used and for what purpose. Demonstrate how, for this game, they should roll the dice and look at the key to find out which piece of measuring equipment they must use, and then find a corresponding question that could be answered using that piece of equipment.

SUGGESTED QUESTIONS:

- Which piece of equipment would be best for answering this question?
- Why do you think that?

Woolly jumpers (page 43)

Provide each child with some string and a ruler. Encourage them to make an estimate of the length of the wool first before measuring with the string.

SUGGESTED QUESTION/PROMPT:

- About how long do you think this piece of wool is?
- Explain how the string and ruler can be used to help you check your estimate.

DIY tape measure (page 44)

It is important that children have plenty of experience in measuring with rulers, metre sticks and tape measures. They can use their tape measures to find (and record) the lengths of a range of different things, for example parts of the body, plants, trees, vegetables in the school grounds, etc.

SUGGESTED QUESTIONS:

- Is your wrist smaller than your ankle?
- By how much?
- How much less than 1 metre is the length around your head?

Pyramid picture (page 45)

At the start of the lesson, discuss the methods that the children use when estimating lengths and distances. Ask them to suggest things that they can compare lengths less than 1 m to, for example a finger is about 1 cm wide, a hand is about 15 cm long.

SUGGESTED QUESTION:

- How close was your estimate?

Game show (page 46)

This activity can be used as an assessment to see how comfortable the children are with the units of measurement, i.e. centimetres, metres, grams, kilograms, litres and millilitres.

SUGGESTED QUESTION:

- Have you given the same answers as your partner?

Read, to the nearest division and half-division, scales that are numbered or partially numbered; use the information to measure and draw to a suitable degree of accuracy

It is important that children become familiar with different types of scales on a range of measuring instruments and begin to learn how to interpret the reading. Initially, children should read from scales where all divisions are numbered and then should move on to those where the interval marks are shown but not numbered. This requires them to work out what each unnumbered mark represents. As they first encounter this work, the unnumbered marks represent one unit and the numbered divisions may go up in twos, fives or tens, leading towards numbered intervals of 100 or 200. Another aspect of reading scales is realising that amounts can be slightly above or below a mark. Vocabulary such as 'about', 'almost', 'just under', 'just over' is also important for children of this age.

Children of this age should confidently use rulers to draw and measure different lengths of line (to the nearest half-centimetre).

Rulers rule (page 47)

Show the children a 30 cm ruler and explain that the worksheet shows pictures of rulers like this.

SUGGESTED QUESTIONS:

- How long is this lizard?
- Is it just over or just under 21 cm, or is it exactly 21 cm?

Cookery class (page 48)

Hold up a real kitchen timer and discuss what they are used for. Then look at the worksheet and point out that only every tenth division is numbered.

SUGGESTED QUESTIONS:

- Does this timer show 21 minutes?
- How many minutes does this timer show?

Kitchen scales (page 49)

This worksheet requires the children to draw arrows onto each set of kitchen scales to match the mass given. Encourage the children to check each other's answers.

SUGGESTED QUESTIONS:

- What does this scale show?
- Where does the arrow go to show this weight?

Measuring jugs (page 50)

Provide each child with a blue coloured pencil and hold up a jug that holds 1000 ml to give children experience of how much liquid is being described on the sheet. For the extension activity remind them that there are 1000 ml in 1 litre.

SUGGESTED QUESTIONS:

- Where on this scale does 250 ml come?
- Which two multiples of 100 does it lie between?
- Is it half way between them?

Thirsty work (page 51)

These cards can be used for a range of games and activities.

- **Game 1** The cards are placed face down on the table. The children, in pairs, pick two cards each and find the totals of the two amounts. The player with the larger amount of liquid scores a point. The cards are returned to the table and the game continues.
- **Game 2** The cards are placed face down on the table. The children, in pairs, pick two cards each and find the differences between the two amounts. The player with the smaller difference scores a point.
- **Game 3** The children, in pairs, pick a card each and say how much more or less than 1 litre their amount is. The player with the amount closest to 1 litre scores a point.
- **Game 4** The cards are placed face down. A target amount is chosen and the children pick a card each and see who has the amount closest to the chosen target.
  - Individual children can pick two cards, read the scale and say which shows the largest amount and record them using the < or > signs.
  - More confident children can write the amounts in different ways, such as in litres, in millilitres, or in both.

- How did you know that this jug holds 650 ml?
- What method did you use to work out that 80 ml is 920 ml less than 1 litre?

Crack the code: 1 and 2 (pages 52 and 53)

This activity provides opportunities for the children to read partially numbered scales. Before the children start on the activity, ask them to explain how they can work out what the unnumbered divisions must stand for on the first scale.

SUGGESTED QUESTIONS:

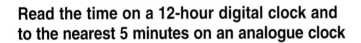

- What does this scale show?
- What unit is this scale measuring?
- Can you think of something that measures/weighs/holds about that amount?

Read the time on a 12-hour digital clock and to the nearest 5 minutes on an analogue clock

As children begin to learn to tell the time to the nearest five minutes on analogue clocks (those with faces), they can begin to be shown how these times are represented by :00, :05, :10 etc. on digital clocks with the hour past preceding the colon.

Time quiz (page 54)

The time quiz game can be played as a whole class activity. Provide each child with a copy of the worksheet and call out clues for times on the worksheet. The children should identify which time you are describing. Clues can be as simple as saying the time in words, or can involve a time interval, for example 20 minutes after ten to five.

SUGGESTED QUESTION/PROMPT:

- How did you know that the time I asked for was 11:20?
- Tell me a way to describe 9:25.

Digital puzzles (page 55)

It is common for children to reverse times, showing ten past five as 10:5, as this matches more closely the way the time is spoken.

SUGGESTED QUESTIONS:

- How did you know that 8:40 is 20 minutes before 9 o'clock?
- Which of the times is 10 minutes before 5:05?

What's the time, Mr Wolf? and Mr Wolf clock cards
(pages 56 and 57)

The clock cards could be copied onto card and the correct times written on the reverse so that children who are less confident with telling the time can check their answers. Point out, however, that there is usually more than one way to

describe a time. If desired, a third child could act as adjudicator during the game.

SUGGESTED QUESTIONS:

- How do you know that this clock shows twenty-five minutes to one?
- Which of the clocks shows the time five to six?

Calculate time intervals and find start or end times for a given time interval

Children should begin to appreciate time intervals, such as saying what time it will be in 25 minutes or three-quarters of an hour, or saying the length of time between two given times.

TV Times: 1 and 2 (pages 58 and 59)

Provide clocks with movable geared hands to help the children with this activity. They should move the hands from one time to the other and work out how long has passed.

SUGGESTED QUESTIONS:

- How long do you have to wait until the cartoons begin?
- How could you say that in a different way?
- How many minutes are between ten to two and half past 2?

Time interval loop cards (page 60)

Provide clocks with movable geared hands to help the children with this activity.

SUGGESTED QUESTIONS:

- What time does this clock show?
- What time would it be 2 hours later/earlier?

At the airport (page 61)

At the start of the lesson, show half past three on a teaching clock with an analogue face. Ask the children what time the clock would have shown 15 minutes before. Repeat for other time intervals.

Provide clocks with movable geared hands to help the children with this worksheet.

SUGGESTED QUESTIONS:

- What time does this clock show?
- How long before it is quarter past three?

The TV race (page 62)

Provide the children with geared analogue clocks to help them work out or check their answers.

SUGGESTED QUESTIONS:

- What time will the programme end?
- How could you check your answer using this clock?

Using the CD-ROM

The PC CD-ROM included with this book contains an easy-to-use software program that allows you to print out pages from the book, to view them (e.g. on an interactive whiteboard) or to customise the activities to suit the needs of your pupils.

Getting started

It's easy to run the software. Simply insert the CD-ROM into your CD drive and the disk should autorun and launch the interface in your web browser.

If the disk does not autorun, open 'My Computer' and select the CD drive, then open the file 'start.html'.

Please note: this CD-ROM is designed for use on a PC. It will also run on most Apple Macintosh computers in Safari however, due to the differences between Mac and PC fonts, you may experience some unavoidable variations in the typography and page layouts of the activity sheets.

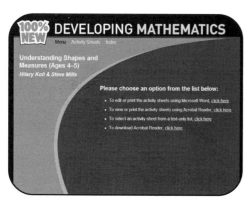

The Menu screen

Four options are available to you from the main menu screen.

The first option takes you to the Activity Sheets screen, where you can choose an activity sheet to edit or print out using Microsoft Word.

(If you do not have the Microsoft Office suite, you might like to consider using OpenOffice instead. This is a multi-platform and multi-lingual office suite, and an 'open-source' project. It is compatible with all other major office suites, and the product is free to download, use and distribute. The homepage for OpenOffice on the Internet is: www.openoffice.org.)

The second option on the main menu screen opens a PDF file of the entire book using Adobe Reader (see below). This format is ideal for printing out copies of the activity sheets or for displaying them, for example on an interactive whiteboard.

The third option allows you to choose a page to edit from a text-only list of the activity sheets, as an alternative to the graphical interface on the Activity Sheets screen.

Adobe Reader is free to download and to use. If it is not already installed on your computer, the fourth link takes you to the download page on the Adobe website.

You can also navigate directly to any of the three screens at any time by using the tabs at the top.

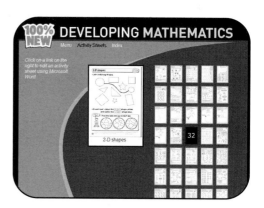

The Activity Sheets screen

This screen shows thumbnails of all the activity sheets in the book. Rolling the mouse over a thumbnail highlights the page number and also brings up a preview image of the page.

Click on the thumbnail to open a version of the page in Microsoft Word (or an equivalent software program, see above.) The full range of editing tools are available to you here to customise the page to suit the needs of your particular pupils. You can print out copies of the page or save a copy of your edited version onto your computer.

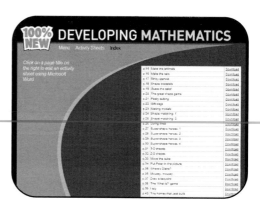

The Index screen

This is a text-only version of the Activity Sheets screen described above. Choose an activity sheet and click on the 'download' link to open a version of the page in Microsoft Word to edit or print out.

Technical support

If you have any questions regarding the *100% New Developing Literacy* or *Developing Mathematics* software, please email us at the address below. We will get back to you as quickly as possible.

educationalsales@acblack.com

Spot the difference

- **Cut out the cards.**
- **Discuss each pair of shapes and say what is** similar **about them and what is** different **.**

Work with a partner.

Look at the length of sides and size of angles.

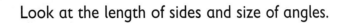

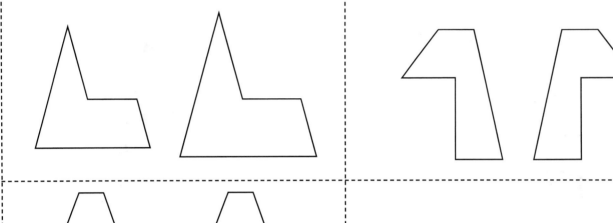

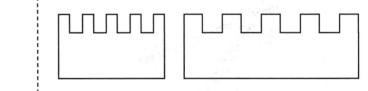

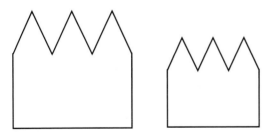

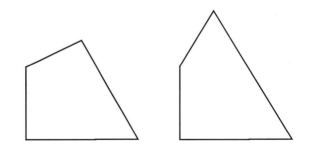

NOW TRY THIS!

- **On a piece of paper, draw four pairs of shapes that are different in some way.**
- **Swap with your partner.**
- **Write what is similar and what is different.**

Teachers' note The children should concentrate on one pair of shapes at a time. Encourage them to look at whether the shape has been reflected, enlarged, reduced or stretched in one direction, or whether one vertex has been moved. Ask them to describe the shapes in each pair, looking to see when corresponding sides and angles are the same and when they are different.

100% New Developing Mathematics Understanding Shapes and Measures: Ages 7–8 © A & C BLACK

A sticky situation

1. Arrange three sticks to make a shape. You need matchsticks.

Name the shape.

_____

2. Add two more sticks, without moving the first three.

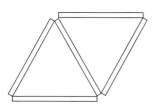

(a) How many sides? ____

(b) Name the shape.

_____

3. Add two more sticks, without moving the others.
Draw the shape.

(a) How many sides? ____

(b) Name the shape.

_____

4. Add two more sticks, without moving the others.
Draw the shape.

(a) How many sides? ____

(b) Name the shape.

_____

5. Add two more sticks, without moving the others.
Draw the shape.

(a) How many sides? ____

(b) Name the shape.

_____

Teachers' note The children do not need to consider the sticks in the centre of the shape when counting sides or naming the shape. Ensure that all shapes are closed and that sticks join end to end without gaps. Ask the children to compare their work with others, as different shapes are possible. They could continue adding two sticks at a time, recording on the back of the sheet.

100% New Developing Mathematics
Understanding Shapes and
Measures: Ages 7–8
© A & C BLACK

14

Stargazer

- ## Follow these instructions.

☆ Use a **green** pencil to join three stars to make a triangle with equal sides.

☆ Use a **blue** pencil to join four stars to make a symmetrical shape with no right angles.

☆ Use a **red** pencil to join five stars to make a pentagon that has two right angles.

☆ Use a **black** pencil to join four stars to make a square.

Use straight lines to join the stars.

NOW TRY THIS!

- ## Make up a stargazer puzzle for a partner to try.

Teachers' note For the extension activity, provide tracing paper. The children can draw some stars on paper and then use tracing paper to join some of them to make shapes which they should then describe. These clues can be given to a partner so that he/she can hunt for the hidden shapes.

100% New Developing Mathematics Understanding Shapes and Measures: Ages 7–8
© A & C BLACK

Draw and name game

- ## Play this game with a partner.
- ## Draw and name...

You need a counter, a ruler, a pencil and some paper each, and a dice to share.

Start	a shape with four sides	a shape with three straight sides	a symmetrical shape	a shape with four right angles

a shape that has one curved side	a shape with ten straight sides	a shape that has five sides and one right angle	a shape that is half a circle
a shape with four lines of symmetry	**Finish** a shape that has seven straight sides		a shape that has three sides and one right angle
a shape with four equal sides	a shape with three equal sides	a shape with three lines of symmetry	a shape with one line of symmetry
a shape with one right angle	a shape with three right angles	a symmetrical shape with six sides	a shape that has four sides and two right angles
a shape with six straight sides	a shape with more than four sides	a shape that has six sides and one right angle	a shape with five straight sides
a shape that is **not** symmetrical	a shape with eight straight sides	a shape with two lines of symmetry	a shape with no right angles

Teachers' note The children take turns to throw the dice and move their counter. As each child lands on a section of the trail he/she should draw a shape that matches the description. If the shape is drawn correctly he/she gets one point. A second point can be gained if the child can also name the shape. The winner is the player with the most points at the finish line.

100% New Developing Mathematics
Understanding Shapes and
Measures: Ages 7–8
© A & C BLACK

Building work

- **Build each shape.**
- **Write how many cubes you used for each shape.**

> **You need** interlocking cubes.

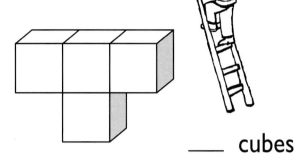

1.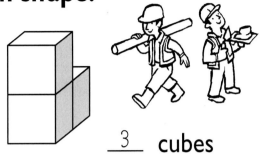

_3_ **cubes**

2.

___ **cubes**

3.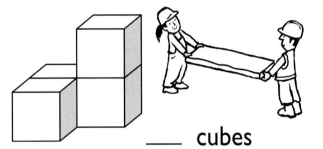

___ **cubes**

4.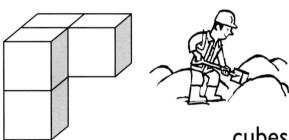

___ **cubes**

5.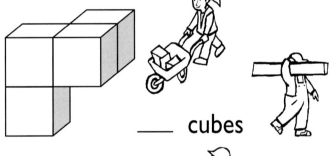

___ **cubes**

6.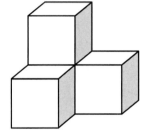

___ **cubes**

7.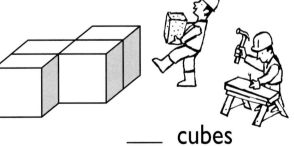

___ **cubes**

8.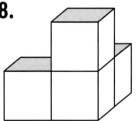

___ **cubes**

NOW TRY THIS!

- **Talk to a partner about which of the shapes above are the same.**

Teachers' note As a further extension, the children could colour the shapes on the worksheet to match the models they have made. This can help them to appreciate where some cubes are not seen at all or where only one or two of their faces are visible.

100% New Developing Mathematics Understanding Shapes and Measures: Ages 7–8 © A & C BLACK

Traffic lights

- **Colour the three sets of traffic lights, like this:**

  You need red, orange and green coloured pencils.

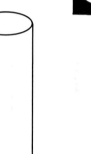

- **Now find the shape that matches each description.**
- **Colour the solid shape to match the traffic light.**

1.

It has a square face.

It has six vertices.

It has a curved face.

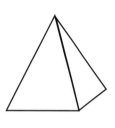 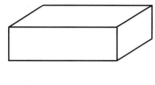 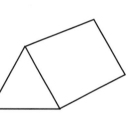 

2.

It has a circular face.

It has eight vertices.

It has nine edges.

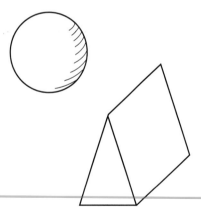 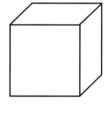 

3.

It has two circular faces.

It has one vertex.

It has no flat faces.

 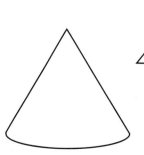 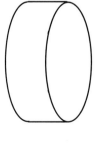 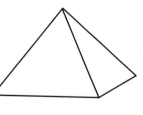

Teachers' note Before the children begin the activity, ensure that they have coloured each set of traffic lights correctly (you could colour the example at the top of the sheet before giving it to the children). Provide the children with matching solid shapes to enable them to count and examine the properties. As an extension, ask the children to name the three red shapes.

100% New Developing Mathematics Understanding Shapes and Measures: Ages 7–8 © A & C BLACK

Shape all-sorts

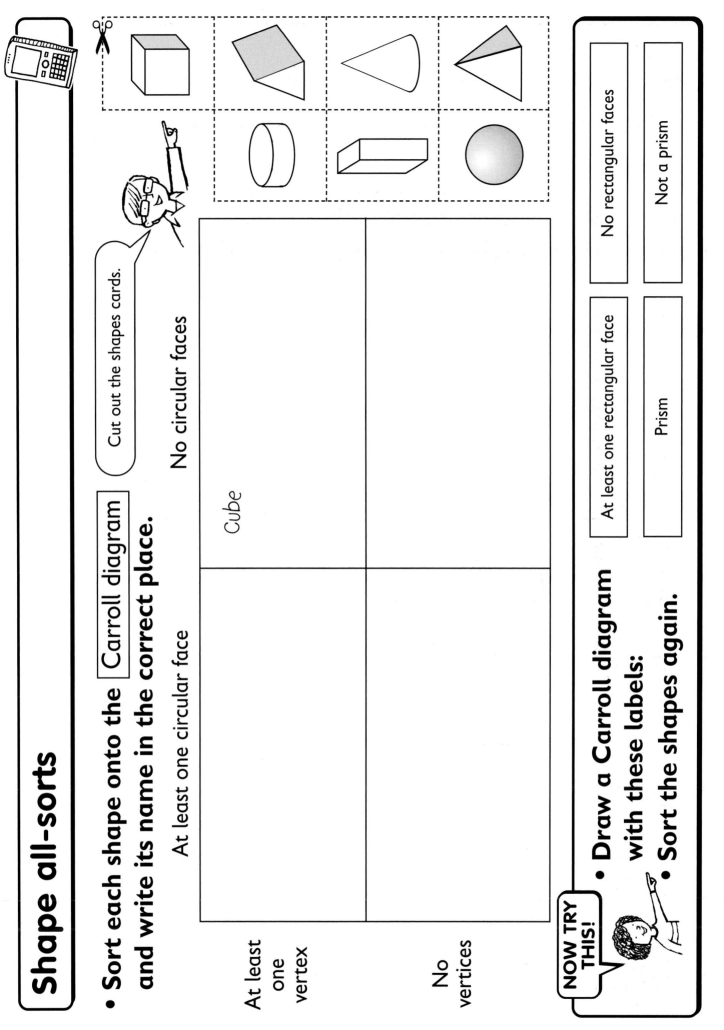

- **Sort each shape onto the** Carroll diagram **and write its name in the correct place.**

Cut out the shapes cards.

	No circular faces	At least one circular face
At least one vertex	Cube	
No vertices		

Teachers' note Ensure that the children know how to complete a Carroll diagram by demonstrating simple sorting with coloured 2-D shapes, for example red, not red, square, not square. For the extension activity, discuss that rectangles include squares and that prisms can include cubes, cuboids and cylinders as each has the same cross-section throughout its length.

**100% New Developing Mathematics
Understanding Shapes and
Measures: Ages 7–8
© A & C BLACK**

Taboo or not taboo

☆ Take turns to secretly pick a shape from the grid.

☆ Describe the shape to the others in your group.

☆ You must **not** say the name of the shape or name the shapes of the faces.

Work in a group of three or four.

 Words you CANNOT use

sphere, cube, cuboid, cone, cylinder, prism, pyramid, hemisphere

square, circle, triangle, rectangle, hexagon, pentagon

Some words you CAN use

solid, faces, vertex, vertices, edges, surface

curved, straight, flat, equal

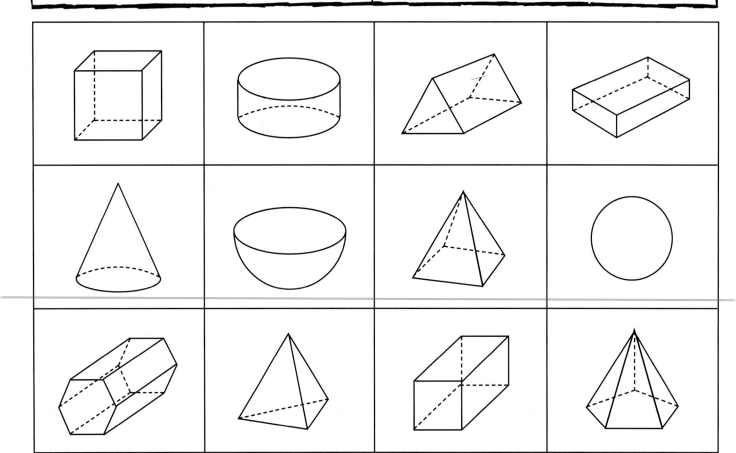

 **NOW TRY THIS!**

• **Now each write a description of one shape, giving as much detail as you can.**

Teachers' note The 'listeners' must monitor whether any taboo words have been spoken, whilst trying to work out from the description which shape is being described. For the extension activity, remind children that they can't use the names of the shapes.

20

100% New Developing Mathematics
Understanding Shapes and
Measures: Ages 7–8
© A & C BLACK

Symmetry Cemetery

- **In Symmetry Cemetery, all the gravestones must be** symmetrical **.**

- **Tick ✔ the gravestones that are allowed in the cemetery and cross ✗ the ones that are not.**

- **Using a ruler, draw the lines of symmetry.**

One has been done for you.

✔

Teachers' note Ensure the children appreciate that the lines of symmetry do not need to be vertical in order for the gravestone to be allowed into the cemetery. As a further extension, the children could draw five more gravestones on the back of this sheet. They could then ask a partner to say whether these gravestones would be allowed in Symmetry Cemetery.

100% New Developing Mathematics Understanding Shapes and Measures: Ages 7–8 © A & C BLACK

Shape symmetry

• **Draw the** reflection **of each shape in the dotted mirror line.**

One has been done for you. Use a ruler.

1.

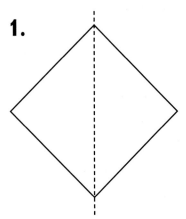

2.

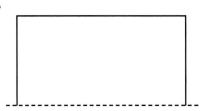

3.

4.

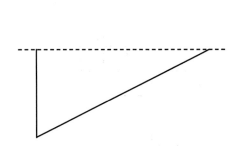

5.

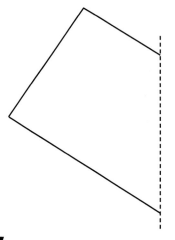

6.

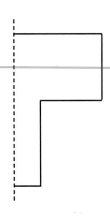

7.

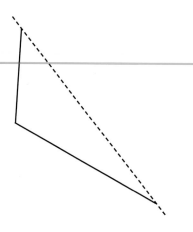

NOW TRY THIS!

• **Under each shape, write the name of the new shape you have made.**

Teachers' note Provide the children with mirrors and demonstrate how they should be used to help draw and check reflections. In this activity, the children place their mirrors along the dotted line (which is one side of the shape). If preferred, the children could use tracing paper to check reflections or help them to draw the shapes more accurately.

100% New Developing Mathematics Understanding Shapes and Measures: Ages 7–8
© A & C BLACK

Mosaic patterns

Each pattern is made from small tiles.

- Shade **<u>two tiles</u>** to make each pattern | symmetrical |.

One pattern has been done for you.

1.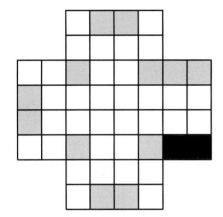

2.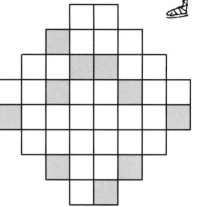

3.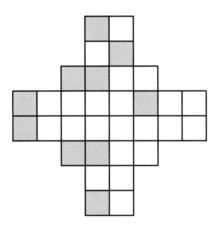

4.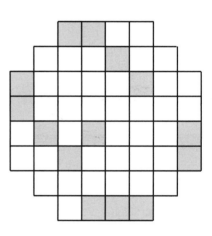

5.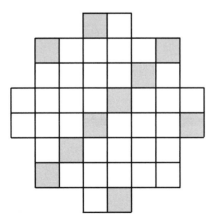

6.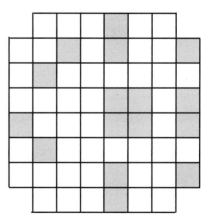

NOW TRY THIS!

- **Now colour some of the patterns.**

Make sure you keep them symmetrical.

Teachers' note This activity involves lines of symmetry in different orientations, including where the lines are diagonal. All patterns have only one line of symmetry. Provide children with mirrors to test and check their reflections (see page 7). Encourage children to draw in the lines of symmetry to help them if necessary.

**100% New Developing Mathematics
Understanding Shapes and
Measures: Ages 7–8
© A & C BLACK**

Secret symmetry

• **Play this game with a partner.**

☆ First make a **symmetrical** pattern by drawing 20 spots on this grid. Two have been done for you.

 Keep your pattern secret.

My pattern

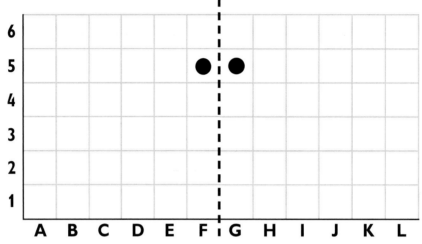

☆ Take turns to say the position of a square on the grid (such as B4).

☆ The other player must say whether he/she has a spot in that square.

If the answer is 'yes', record the spot on the grid below and have another go.
If the answer is 'no', it's the other player's turn.

The other player's pattern

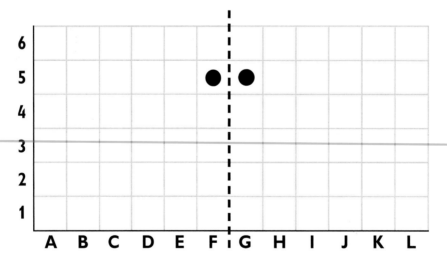

☆ The first person to work out the other player's pattern is the winner.

NOW TRY THIS!

• **Colour some empty squares in the grid above.**

Make sure the patterns are still symmetrical.

Teachers' note Give each child a copy of this sheet. The children will need a screen, for example a large book or a folder, to hide their patterns from their partners'. Encourage the children to mark with crosses those squares they have found that do **not** contain spots.

100% New Developing Mathematics Understanding Shapes and Measures: Ages 7–8
© A & C BLACK

Dotty symmetry

• Draw the $\boxed{\text{reflection}}$ of each shape in the mirror line.

NOW TRY THIS!

• Use a mirror to check your reflections.

Teachers' note Provide the children with mirrors and demonstrate how they should be used to help draw and check reflections. For the extension activity, encourage the children to turn the sheet round to make the mirror lines vertical or horizontal.

**100% New Developing Mathematics
Understanding Shapes and
Measures: Ages 7–8
© A & C BLACK**

25

Lost!

☆ This is a game for 2 to 4 players. **You need** a small counter each.

☆ Cut out the direction cards. Place them face down on the table.

☆ Each place a counter on a 'Start' square.

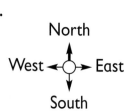

☆ Take turns to pick a card and move one square in the direction shown. Replace the card. If you land on 'Pick again' or your move will take you off the edge of the board, pick another card.

☆ The winner is the first to reach a 'Finish!' square.

Finish!							**Finish!**
		Pick again			Pick again		
Pick again			**Start**	**Start**			Pick again
	Pick again		**Start**	**Start**		Pick again	
		Pick again			Pick again		
Finish!							**Finish!**

N	N	N	S	S	S
E	E	E	W	W	W

Teachers' note If possible, enlarge the worksheet to A3 size. Encourage the children to place the cards in a pile face down on the table and, as they use the cards, to replace them at the bottom of the pile. Some children might find it easier to play with a counter that has an arrow marked on it. They can then move the arrow to face the direction in which they are moving.

100% New Developing Mathematics Understanding Shapes and Measures: Ages 7–8 © A & C BLACK

Dodge the dangers

☆ **You need** a small counter to place on the 'Start' square.

☆ Move to the 'Finish' square, dodging all the dangers.

☆ Write three different routes in the table below.

☆ Use these letters: N S E W

North

West ◄─◆─► East

South

							Finish
Start		DANGER					

	Route 1	Route 2	Route 3
	E1		
	N2		

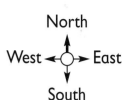

NOW TRY THIS!

• **Draw route 3 on the grid.**

• **On a sheet of paper, write the instructions to route 3, going backwards from** Finish **to** Start **.**

Teachers' note A game for two players can be played with this 'maze'. Give pairs of children a set of cards marked N, S, E and W (cut from page 26) and a counter each. The children take turns to pick a card and, where possible, move in that direction until a danger is reached. A target square can be agreed in advance and the winner is the first to reach it.

100% New Developing Mathematics
Understanding Shapes and
Measures: Ages 7–8
© A & C BLACK

Lawnmower man

The gardener at a football ground mows the grass very strangely.

- Describe his route across the pitch using the compass points.

One has been done for you.

N
W ← → E
S

1.

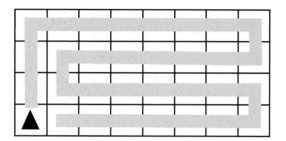

N3, E7, S1, W6, S1, E6, S1, W6 _____

_____

2.

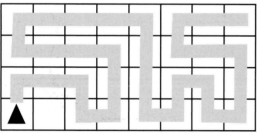

_____

_____

_____

3.

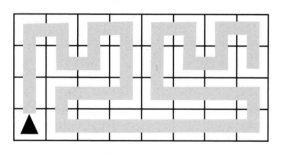

_____

_____

_____

4.

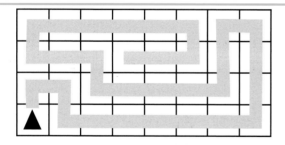

_____

_____

_____

Teachers' note To help the children work out how far to travel in any direction, encourage them to work from the centre of a square and count the number of positions moved to other centres of squares. It can help to draw dots in the centre of each square to help with the count.

100% New Developing Mathematics Understanding Shapes and Measures: Ages 7–8
© A & C BLACK

A counter is placed on a square and then moved.

• **Write where the counter ends up each time.**

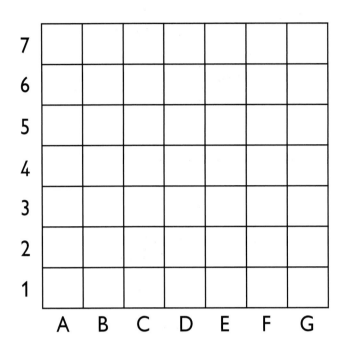

1. | The counter is put on D3. It is moved 2 squares East and 4 squares North. | It is now on ☐

2. | The counter is put on F6. It is moved 4 squares South and 2 squares West. | It is now on ☐

3. | The counter is put on A4. It is moved 3 squares North and 5 squares East. | It is now on ☐

4. | The counter is put on G5. It is moved 6 squares West and 2 squares South. | It is now on ☐

5. | The counter is put on E1. It is moved 4 squares North and 3 squares West. | It is now on ☐

NOW TRY THIS!

• **Make up three puzzles of your own for a partner to solve.**

Teachers' note Remind the children of the directions North, South, East and West at the start of the lesson.

100% New Developing Mathematics Understanding Shapes and Measures: Ages 7–8
© A & C BLACK

Map work

- **Complete each sentence using numbers and the directions**
  North , South , East , **or** West .

You need a ruler.

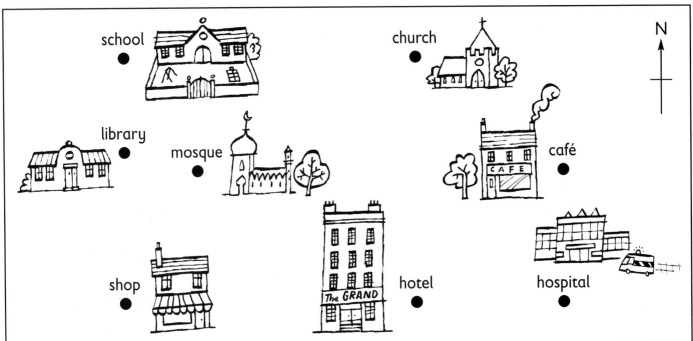

school

church

N

library

mosque

café

C A F E

shop

The GRAND

hotel

hospital

- **On the map:**

1. the church is | 8 | cm | East | of the school

2. the shop is | | cm | | of the hospital

3. the library is | | cm | | of the school

4. the library is | | cm | | of the shop

5. the hospital is | | cm | | of the cafe

6. the café is | | cm | | of the mosque

NOW TRY THIS!

- **Write four more sentences of your own about the map.**

Teachers' note Encourage the children to measure from dot to dot rather than from word to word. For the extension activity, the children could find distances and directions between places on the map, eg. the shop and church. As a further extension, the children could draw their own maps on squared paper and write sentences about them.

**100% New Developing Mathematics
Understanding Shapes and
Measures: Ages 7–8**
© A & C BLACK

Learner driver

- **Mark all the** right angles **in this picture.**
- **Use the 'L' shape to help you check each angle.**

Teachers' note If necessary, explain to the children that people learning to drive have to stick an 'L' sign on their car when they are driving. As an extension, the children could draw their own picture with as many right angles in it as they can. Some children could use the right angle symbol ⌐ if they are ready to.

100% New Developing Mathematics
Understanding Shapes and
Measures: Ages 7–8
© A & C BLACK

It's your turn!

The first tile in the row is turned.

• Tick ✔ the picture which shows the correct turn.

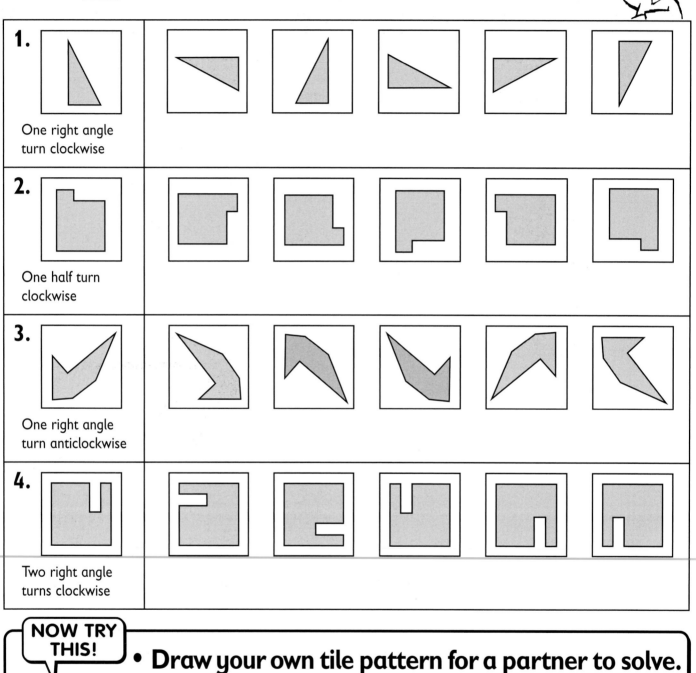

1. One right angle turn clockwise

2. One half turn clockwise

3. One right angle turn anticlockwise

4. Two right angle turns clockwise

NOW TRY THIS!

• **Draw your own tile pattern for a partner to solve.**

One right angle turn clockwise

Teachers' note At the start of the lesson, demonstrate turning clockwise and anticlockwise through a number of right angles (see page 8). If necessary, the children could cut out the first tile in each row and turn it to match the description to see which picture it matches. Alternatively they could trace the tile.

**100% New Developing Mathematics
Understanding Shapes and
Measures: Ages 7–8
© A & C BLACK**

Learning about turning

Jo faces the first letter of each word and turns
to face the next letter. For each word, her turn is:

| less than a right angle | **or** | a right angle | **or** | more than a right angle |

- **Write each word under the correct heading below to
  show what kind of turn Jo has made.**

AM	AN
GO	ME
IS	BE
BY	AT
AS	OH
HE	ON
MY	TO
IN	HI
IT	SO

less than a right angle	a right angle	more than a right angle

Teachers' note For this activity, the children can decide whether to turn clockwise or anticlockwise for
each turn. Encourage them to discuss their answers with a partner and to justify any disagreements.
At the end of the lesson, discuss how a turn clockwise and a different turn anticlockwise can produce
the same result.

100% New Developing Mathematics
Understanding Shapes and
Measures: Ages 7–8
© A & C BLACK

Angle art

Some angles are marked with an arc .

• **Colour:**

– angles smaller than a right angle **yellow**,

– right angles **red**,

– angles larger than a right angle **blue**.

You need
yellow, red and blue coloured pencils.

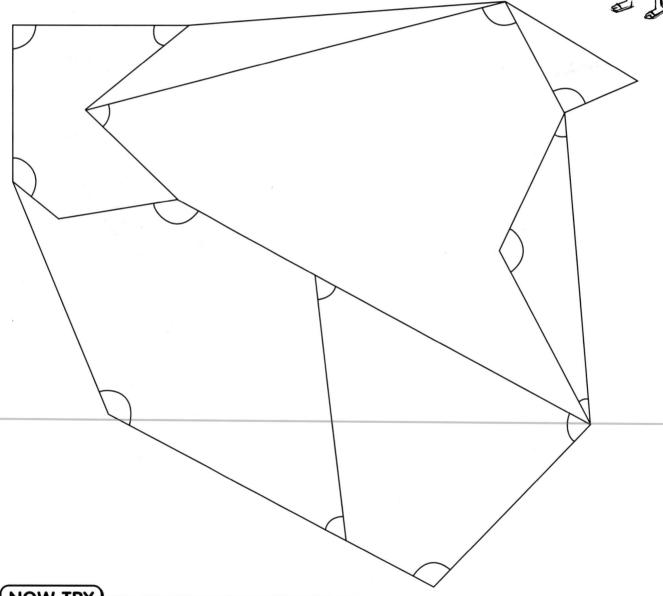

NOW TRY THIS!

• **Now use the same colours to colour the angles that are <u>not</u> marked with arcs.**

Teachers' note The children could be given a set-square or a right angle tester (such as the right angle gobbler from page 35) to help them complete this activity, or to help them check their answers. Discuss with the children who tackle the extension activity what they notice about the size of most of the angles outside the shape.

**100% New Developing Mathematics
Understanding Shapes and
Measures: Ages 7–8
© A & C BLACK**

Birds' beaks

• Work with a partner.

☆ Look at the angle of each beak.

☆ Say what size you think it is.

☆ Use the right angle gobbler to check.

It looks about one-third of a right angle.

Mmm.

NOW TRY THIS!

- **Cut out the birds.**
- **Put the angles of the beaks in order, smallest to largest.**

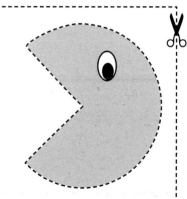

Teachers' note Children find the concept of angle very difficult and can wrongly confuse angle with the length of the beak or the distance between the two end-points of the line. Encourage them to describe the size of the angles in relation to a right angle, for example 'I think this looks about one-third of a right angle'.

100% New Developing Mathematics Understanding Shapes and Measures: Ages 7–8 © A & C BLACK

Stream scheme

Scientists are measuring the depth of water in a stream at different times in the year.

- **The measurements are written in metres. Change them to centimetres.**

1. 4 m = $\boxed{400}$ cm

2. 7 m = ☐ cm

3. 2 m = ☐ cm

4. 3 m = ☐ cm

5. 1 m = ☐ cm

6. $\frac{1}{2}$ m = ☐ cm

7. $\frac{1}{10}$ m = ☐ cm

8. $6\frac{1}{2}$ m = ☐ cm

9. 25 m = ☐ cm

10. 10 m = ☐ cm

11. $\frac{1}{4}$ m = ☐ cm

12. $\frac{3}{4}$ m = ☐ cm

NOW TRY THIS!

- **Change these measurements to metres and centimetres.**

(a) 518 cm = $\boxed{5}$ m $\boxed{18}$ cm

(b) 900 cm = ☐ m ☐ cm

(c) 150 cm = ☐ m ☐ cm

(d) 350 cm = ☐ m ☐ cm

(e) 125 cm = ☐ m ☐ cm

(f) 375 cm = ☐ m ☐ cm

(g) 120 cm = ☐ m ☐ cm

(h) 70 cm = ☐ m ☐ cm

Teachers' note Ensure that the children understand the abbreviations 'cm' and 'm', and that 100 cm is equal to 1 m. The numbers on this worksheet could be altered for differentiation.

100% New Developing Mathematic
Understanding Shapes and Measures: Ages 7–8
© A & C BLACK

Ribbons

A shop sells lots of different ribbons.
These ribbons measure [1 metre].
• **Write how much ribbon is left
  if some is cut off.**

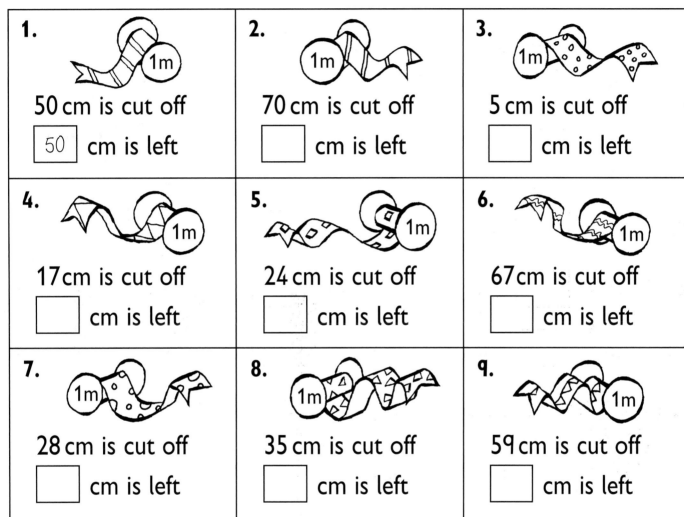

1.
50 cm is cut off
[50] cm is left

2.
70 cm is cut off
[   ] cm is left

3.
5 cm is cut off
[   ] cm is left

4.
17 cm is cut off
[   ] cm is left

5.
24 cm is cut off
[   ] cm is left

6.
67 cm is cut off
[   ] cm is left

7.
28 cm is cut off
[   ] cm is left

8.
35 cm is cut off
[   ] cm is left

9.
59 cm is cut off
[   ] cm is left

NOW TRY THIS!

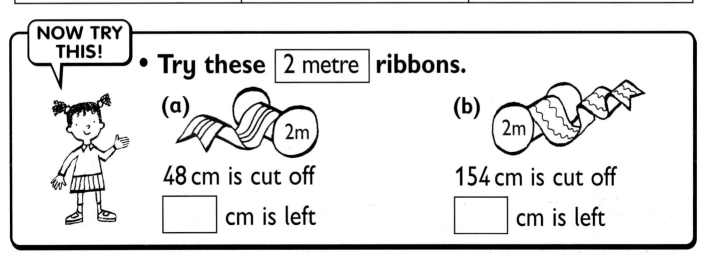

• **Try these [2 metre] ribbons.**

(a)
48 cm is cut off
[   ] cm is left

(b)
154 cm is cut off
[   ] cm is left

Teachers' note Begin the lesson by practising number pairs that total 100 (see page 9) as knowledge of these are required for the activity. The children could use the tape measure from page 44 to help them with this activity.

**100% New Developing Mathematics
Understanding Shapes and
Measures: Ages 7–8**
© A & C BLACK

How far?

This map shows how far from school some children live.

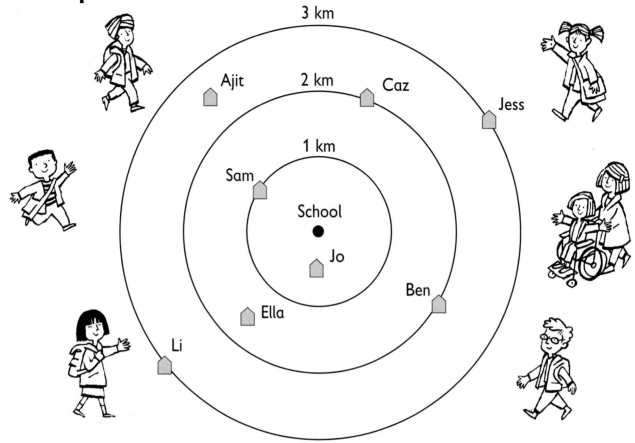

- **Tick** ✔ **to show whether each statement is** `true` **or** `false`.

	true	false
1. Sam lives about 1000 m from school.	☐	☐
2. Jess lives about 300 m from school.	☐	☐
3. Ben lives about 2000 m from school.	☐	☐
4. Li lives about 3000 m from school.	☐	☐
5. Jo lives about 500 m from school.	☐	☐
6. Ajit lives about 2500 m from school.	☐	☐

NOW TRY THIS!

- **Write** `true` **statements to say how far from school Caz and Ella live.** (Use metres.)

Teachers' note At the start of the lesson ensure that the children understand the abbreviations 'm' and 'km', and that 1000 m is equal to 1 km. Discuss how far this distance is in relation to the school. Explain how the diagram works by showing, with a piece of string, how all the points that are the same distance from the school form a circle.

100% New Developing Mathematics Understanding Shapes and Measures: Ages 7–8
© A & C BLACK

Weight lifters

- **For each weight lifter, colour both weights if they are the same.**

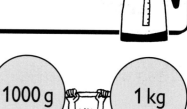

1000 g   1 kg

1.

3000 g   3 kg

2.

200 g   2 kg

3.

500 g $\frac{1}{2}$ kg

4.

6000 g   6 kg

5.

4000 g   4 kg

6.

3 g   300 kg

7.

500 g   0·5 kg

8.

2500 g   2·5 kg

9.

3·5 g   3500 kg

10.

1500 g   1·5 kg

11.

250 g $\frac{1}{4}$ kg

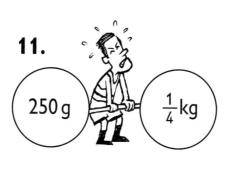

12.

1250 g $1\frac{1}{4}$ kg

NOW TRY THIS!

- **On the back of this sheet, draw three more weight lifters with weights that are equal amounts.**

Teachers' note Ensure that the children understand the abbreviations 'g' and 'kg', and that 1000 g is equal to 1 kg. Encourage them to look out for the correct units and to look closely at the numbers to see whether the measurements are equivalent. The numbers could be altered for further differentiation.

100% New Developing Mathematics Understanding Shapes and Measures: Ages 7–8
© A & C BLACK

Milkshake mistakes

These children are making milkshakes.
- Tick ✔ to show who is right each time.

1. This is the same as 10 litres. ☐ **1000 ml** No, it's the same as 1 litre. ✔

2. This is the same as $\frac{1}{2}$ litre. ☐ **500 ml** No, it's the same as 5 litres. ☐

3. This is the same as 2 litres. ☐ **2000 ml** No, it's the same as $\frac{1}{2}$ litre. ☐

4. This is the same as $1\frac{1}{2}$ litres. ☐ **1500 ml** No, it's the same as 15 litres. ☐

5. This is the same as 25 litres. ☐ **2500 ml** No, it's the same as 2·5 litres. ☐

6. This is the same as 30 litres. ☐ **3000 ml** No, it's the same as 3 litres. ☐

NOW TRY THIS!

- **Try these in the same way.**

(a) This is the same as 50 ml. ☐ **0·5 l** No, it's the same as 500 ml. ☐

(b) This is the same as 3500 ml. ☐ **$3\frac{1}{2}$ l** No, it's the same as 350 ml. ☐

Teachers' note Ensure that the children understand the abbreviations 'ml' and 'l', and that 1000 ml is equal to 1 l. The children may require assistance with interpreting numbers written as decimals or fractions in this activity. The numbers on this worksheet could be altered for differentiation.

100% New Developing Mathematics Understanding Shapes and Measures: Ages 7–8 © A & C BLACK

Question time

- **Cut out the cards.**
- **With a partner, decide which unit of measurement would be the best to use in each answer.**

millimetres	centimetres	metres	kilometres
grams		kilograms	
millilitres		litres	

How far is it to fly from London to Paris? 	How much milk comes from a cow each day?	How heavy is a conker?
How much cough medicine should I take? 	How long is a worm? 	How far do people run in a marathon? 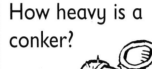
How tall is a giraffe?	How much blood is inside a person? 	How heavy is an elephant? 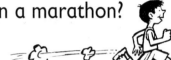
How long is an ant? 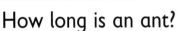 	How much petrol fills the tank in a car? 	How heavy is a blackbird? 
What is the width of a football pitch? 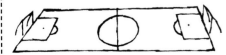	How heavy is a tennis ball? 	How tall is the Eiffel Tower?  

Teachers' note Ensure the children realise that they are not required to answer the questions. The children could write the unit on the back of each card. Discuss other units, such as Imperial units, if they arise, and at the end of the activity, compare and discuss the children's answers. As an extension, the children could write some questions of their own for another pair to discuss.

100% New Developing Mathematics Understanding Shapes and Measures: Ages 7–8
© A & C BLACK

Measure master

☆ Work with a partner. **You need** a dice and counters in two colours.

☆ Take turns to roll the dice and look at the measuring equipment for that dice number.

☆ Match it to a square on the grid and cover the square with a counter in your colour.

☆ The winner is the first to cover four squares in a line.

| ruler | metre stick or tape measure | trundle wheel | weighing scales | measuring jug | stopwatch or egg-timer |

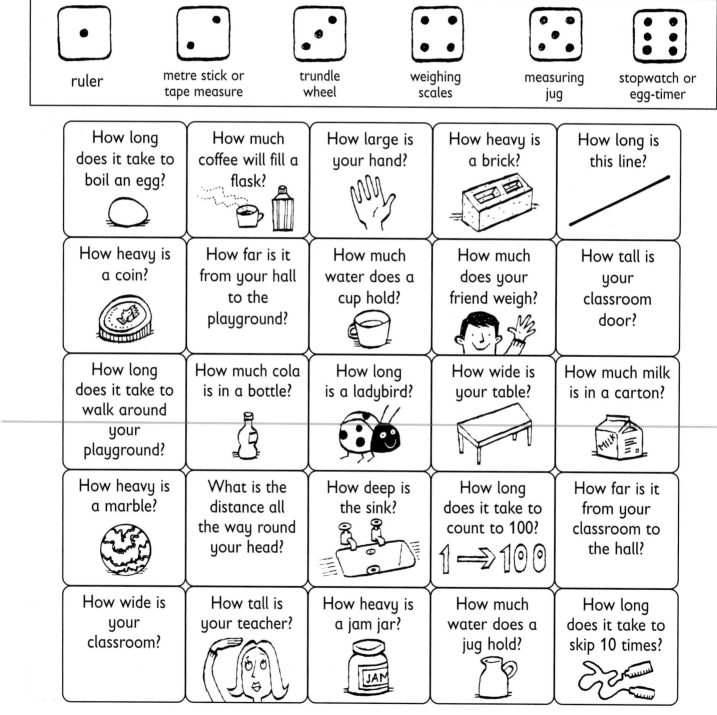

Teachers' note Enlarge this sheet to A3 size for easier use. Ensure the children understand that the piece of measuring equipment must be the most suitable piece of equipment for the situation described on the square. If a player feels that the situation chosen is not most appropriate, they can challenge. The winning line can be horizontal, vertical or diagonal.

100% New Developing Mathematics Understanding Shapes and Measures: Ages 7–8 © A & C BLACK

Woolly jumpers

• **Using a piece of string and a ruler, measure the length of each loose thread.**

Work with a partner.

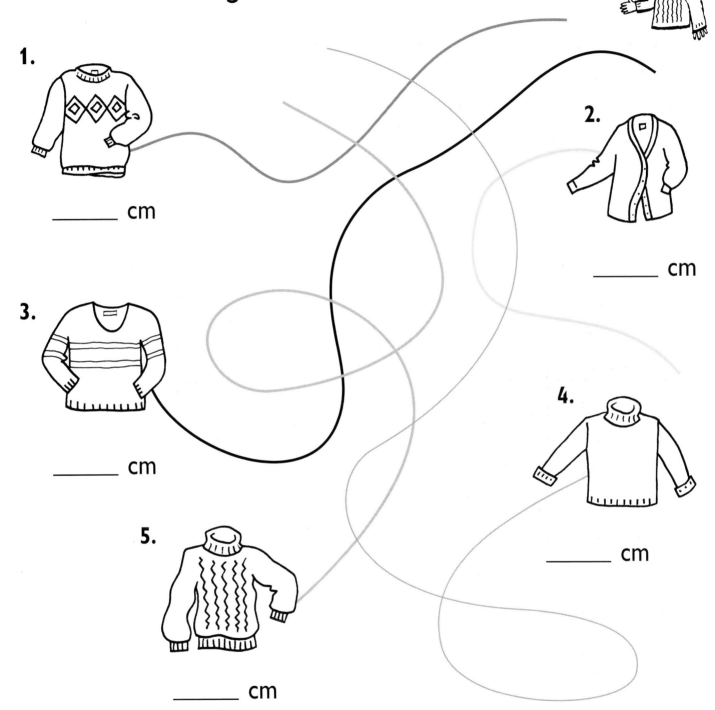

1. _____ cm

2. _____ cm

3. _____ cm

4. _____ cm

5. _____ cm

NOW TRY THIS!

• **On the back of this sheet, draw a jumper with a loose thread that is <u>exactly</u> 24 cm long.**

43

DIY tape measure

- **Cut out the strips and tape them together.**
- **Use your tape measure to find the size of your:**

wrist	elbow	ankle	knee	thigh	waist
0					
1	21	41	61		81
2	22	42	62		82
3	23	43	63		83
4	24	44	64		84
5	25	45	65		85
6	26	46	66		86
7	27	47	67		87
8	28	48	68		88
9	29	49	69		89
10	30	50	70		90
11	31	51	71		91
12	32	52	72		92
13	33	53	73		93
14	34	54	74		94
15	35	55	75		95
16	36	56	76		96
17	37	57	77		97
18	38	58	78		98
19	39	59	79		99
20	40	60	80		1m

Teachers' note The children may need help sticking the strips together with transparent tape or glue. The children should keep their own tape measure (naming it on the reverse) and use it for a range of measuring activities in and around the school, measuring to the nearest centimetre.

**100% New Developing Mathematics
Understanding Shape and
Measures: Ages 7–8**
© A & C BLACK

Pyramid picture

☆ **Estimate** the length of each numbered line.

☆ Write your estimates in the table below.

☆ Then use a ruler to measure the lines and record their lengths.

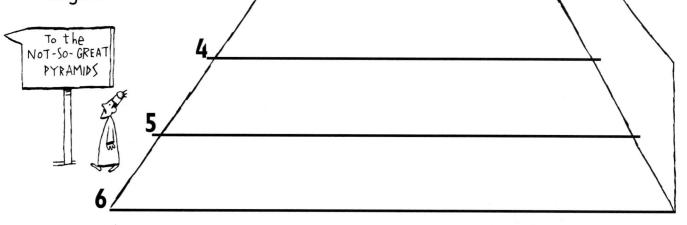

Line	Estimate	Measure
1		
2		
3		
4		
5		
6		

NOW TRY THIS!

• **Add the lengths. Do they total more than 1 m?** _____

• **On the back of this sheet, draw your own pyramid where the lengths come to more than 1 m.**

Teachers' note Encourage the children to accurately measure the lengths of the horizontal lines to the nearest half-centimetre, or if appropriate, to the nearest tenth of a centimetre. For the extension activity, more confident children could try to make the total length of the lines as close to 1 m as they can.

**100% New Developing Mathematics
Understanding Shapes and
Measures: Ages 7–8
© A & C BLACK**

45

Game show

- **Colour the best estimate to win the game show!**

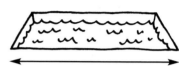

1. The weight of a mobile phone

| 100 g |
| 1 kg |
| 1 g |

2. The length of a swimming pool

| 30 m |
| 3 cm |
| 3 m |

3. The capacity of a wheely bin

| 300 ml |
| 300 l |
| 3 l |

4. The height of a kettle

| 25 m |
| 25 cm |
| 250 m |

5. The weight of a tin of baked bins

| 50 kg |
| 5 g |
| 500 g |

6. The capacity of a jam jar

| 40 l |
| 4 l |
| 400 ml |

7. The depth of a bath

| 400 cm |
| 4 m |
| 40 cm |

8. The width of a door

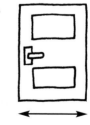

| 70 m |
| 70 cm |
| 700 cm |

NOW TRY THIS!

- **Write three more estimate questions for a partner to solve.**

Teachers' note Have available metre sticks, kilogram and hundred gram weights and measuring containers to help the children to visualise the lengths, masses or capacities more clearly. Encourage the children to compare their answers with a partner and to discuss their reasons.

100% New Developing Mathematics
Understanding Shapes and
Measures: Ages 7–8
© A & C BLACK

Rulers rule

- **Read the** `scale` **on the ruler to find the length of each lizard.**

1. 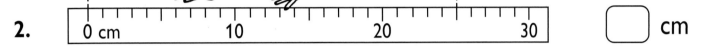 `17` cm

2.  ☐ cm

3.  ☐ cm

4. 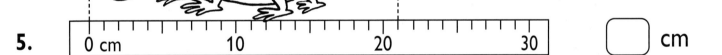 ☐ cm

5.  ☐ cm

6. ☐ cm

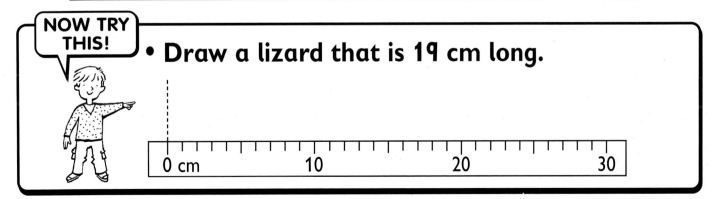

NOW TRY THIS!

- **Draw a lizard that is 19 cm long.**

0 cm   10   20   30

Teachers' note Some children who find this work difficult might benefit from having the sheet enlarged to A3 so that missing numbers can be written onto the scales.

100% New Developing Mathematics
Understanding Shapes and
Measures: Ages 7–8
© A & C BLACK

Cookery class

- **Draw an arrow on each timer to show the correct number of minutes.**

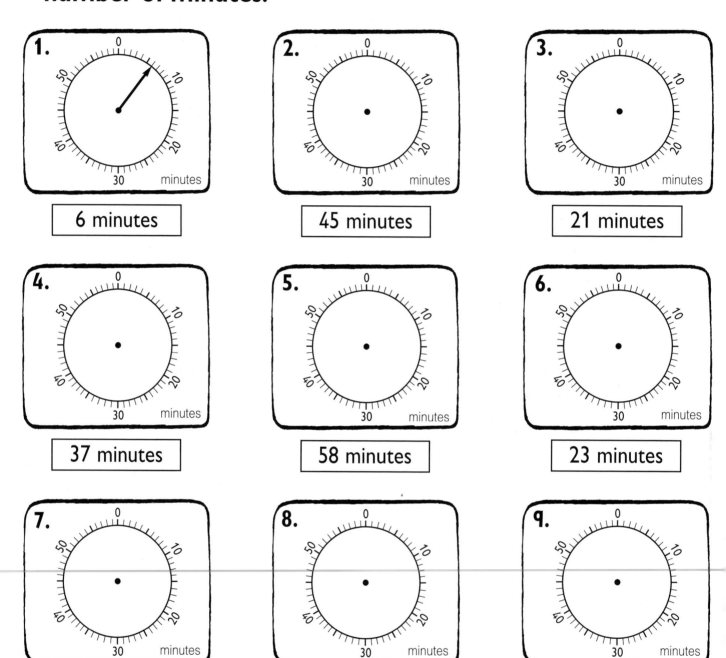

1. 6 minutes

2. 45 minutes

3. 21 minutes

4. 37 minutes

5. 58 minutes

6. 23 minutes

7. 17 minutes

8. 54 minutes

9. 39 minutes

NOW TRY THIS!

- **Under each timer, write how many minutes less than one hour it shows.**

Teachers' note Some children might benefit from the sheet being enlarged to A3 size so that missing numbers can be written onto the scales. Arrows could be drawn on each timer and the numbers removed to provide an alternative activity for practising the reading of scales.

100% New Developing Mathematics Understanding Shapes and Measures: Ages 7–8
© A & C BLACK

Kitchen scales

• **Draw an arrow on the scale to show the weight given.**

2 kg

4 kg 500 g

$6\frac{1}{2}$ kg

500 g

$5\frac{1}{2}$ kg

3 kg 500 g

NOW TRY THIS!

• **Now try these.**

310 g

120 g

290 g

330 g

$\frac{1}{4}$ kg

Teachers' note Some children might benefit from the sheet being enlarged to A3 size so that missing numbers can be written onto the scales.

**100% New Developing Mathematics
Understanding Shapes and
Measures: Ages 7–8
© A & C BLACK**

Measuring jugs

- **Use a blue pencil to show the water level on each jug.**

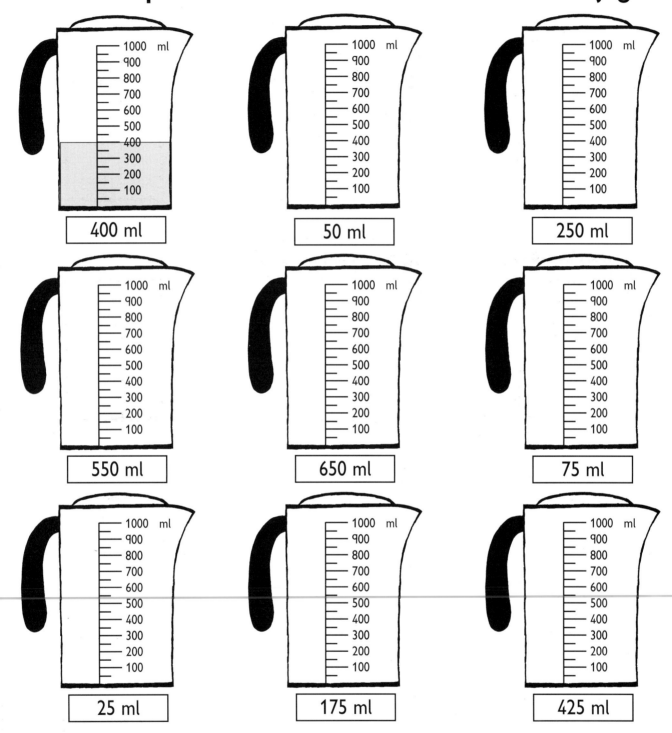

1000 ml ... 100	1000 ml ... 100	1000 ml ... 100
400 ml	**50 ml**	**250 ml**
550 ml	**650 ml**	**75 ml**
25 ml	**175 ml**	**425 ml**

NOW TRY THIS!

- **On a sheet of paper, write how many more millilitres of water are needed in each jug to make 1 litre.**

Teachers' note The measurements can be altered to provide a wider range of variety and practice. For the extension activity, remind the children that 1000 ml is the same as 1 litre.

100% New Developing Mathematics Understanding Shapes and Measures: Ages 7–8
© A & C BLACK

Thirsty work

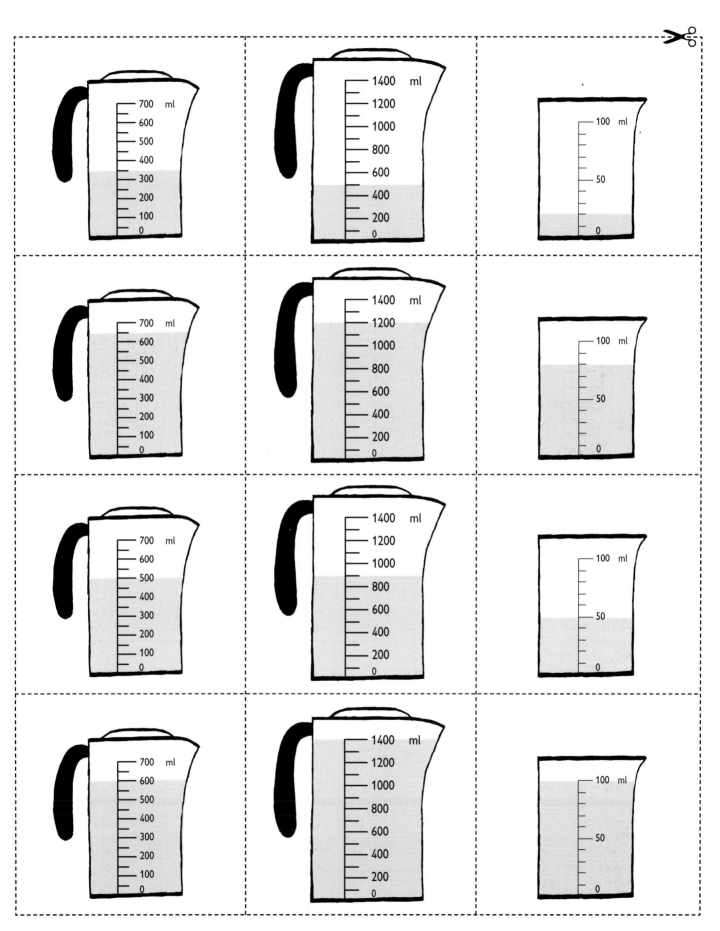

Teachers' note These cards can be used to play three different games. The rules can be found on page 10.

100% New Developing Mathematics
Understanding Shapes and
Measures: Ages 7–8
© A & C BLACK

Crack the code: 1

You need Crack the code: 2.

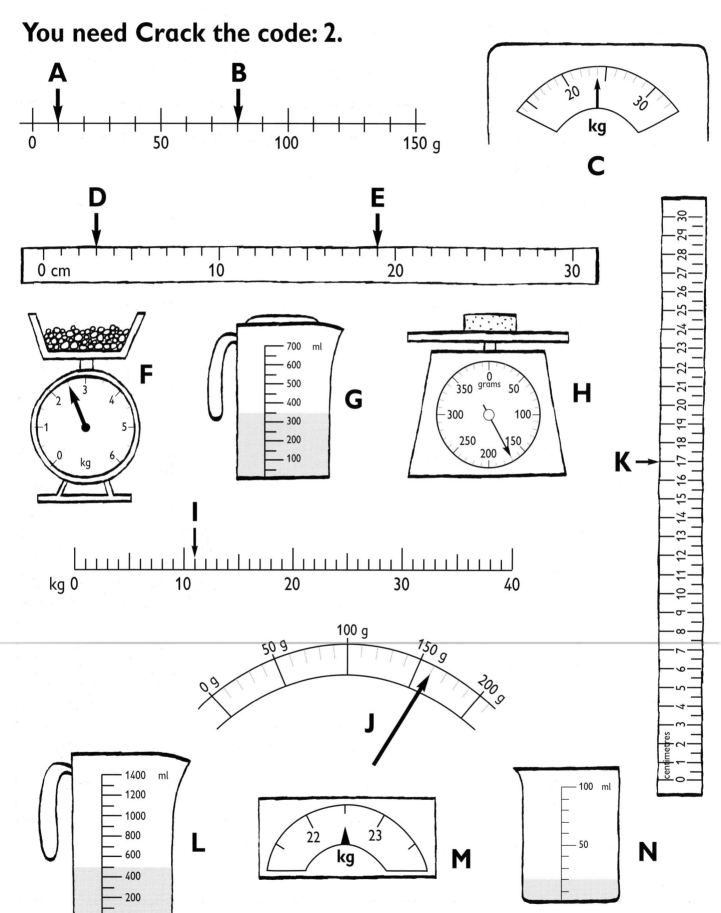

Teachers' note Use this sheet in conjunction with page 53, Crack the code: 2. Some children might benefit from this sheet being enlarged to A3 size so that they can number the intermediate, unnumbered divisions.

**100% New Developing Mathematics
Understanding Shapes and
Measures: Ages 7–8**
© A & C BLACK

• You need Crack the code: 1.

☆ Read the scales and record the answers below.

☆ Find the answers in the key and copy out the matching letter pairs on scrap paper.

☆ When you have worked out what the sentence says, copy it out neatly at the bottom of this sheet.

A | 10 g |

B | |

C | |

D | |

E | |

F | |

G | |

H | |

I | |

J | |

K | |

L | |

M | |

N | |

Key

500 ml	~~10 g~~	24 kg	160 g	19 cm	350 ml	20 ml
ea	~~be~~	gc	yo	er	lk	hy

3 cm	11 kg	80 g	$2\frac{1}{2}$ kg	$22\frac{1}{2}$ kg	17 cm	170 g
he	ps	in	fu	lt	uh	ee

• Copy the sentence here.

be _____

Teachers' note Use this sheet in conjunction with page 52, Crack the code: 1. Encourage the children to cross off each answer as they write the letters in order. If the children have written 2·5 kg rather than $2\frac{1}{2}$ kg, ensure they realise that this is the same measurement.

**100% New Developing Mathematics
Understanding Shapes and
Measures: Ages 7–8**
© A & C BLACK

Time quiz

- **Your teacher has chosen one of these times and will give you some clues.**
- **Can you work out which time has been chosen?**

Teachers' note Instructions for the Time quiz game can be found on page 11. Encourage the children to mark those clocks which do not fit the description with each clue given. Page 55, Digital puzzles, can also be used in conjunction with this sheet to assess how well the children read and interpret digital time.

100% New Developing Mathematics
Understanding Shapes and
Measures: Ages 7–8
© A & C BLACK

Digital puzzles

You need the Time quiz worksheet.

1. Which clock shows ten to two?

`1 : 50`

2. Which clock shows ten past five?

3. Which clock shows quarter to four?

4. Which clock shows twenty to nine?

5. Which time is one hour after quarter past six?

6. Which time is five minutes after half past two?

7. Which time is closest to 11 o'clock?

8. Which time is half an hour after 8:55?

NOW TRY THIS!

- **Write a puzzle for this time:**

11:20

Teachers' note This sheet should be used in conjunction with page 54, Time quiz, as an assessment. It could be altered to provide more challenging questions. As an extension the children could be asked to find pairs of times that are a given period apart, for example 45 minutes (6:30 and 7:15, 1:50 and 2:35, etc).

100% New Developing Mathematics Understanding Shapes and Measures: Ages 7–8
© A & C BLACK

What's the time, Mr Wolf?

- ## Play this game with a partner.

☆ Take turns to roll the dice and move your counter.

☆ If you land on a clock, pick a clock card and say what time it shows. If you get it wrong, move back two places.

☆ If you pick a clock showing 12 o'clock, return to **Start**!

☆ The winner is the first player to reach Mr Wolf.

You need a counter each, a dice and the Mr Wolf clock cards.

Place your Mr Wolf clock cards here.

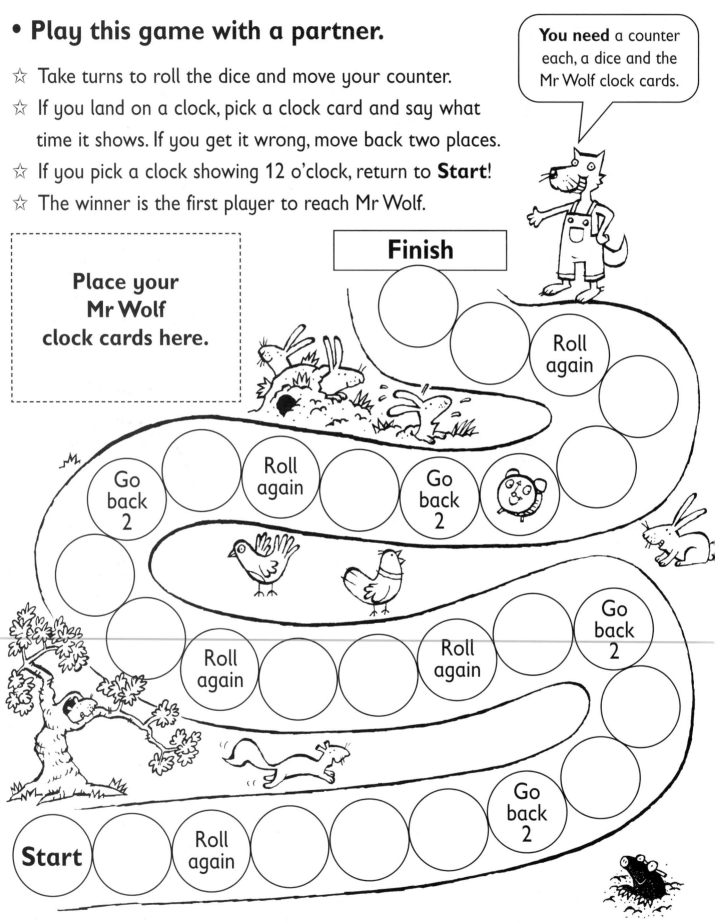

Finish

Roll again

Go back 2

Roll again

Go back 2

Go back 2

Roll again

Roll again

Go back 2

Start

Roll again

Teachers' note Use this sheet in conjunction with page 57, Mr Wolf clock cards. The children need to cut out the Mr Wolf clock cards and place them in a pile. The worksheet can be enlarged to A3 size for easier use. It could also be laminated to create a more permanent resource.

100% New Developing Mathematics Understanding Shapes and Measures: Ages 7–8 © A & C BLACK

Mr Wolf clock cards

• **Cut out the cards.**

Teachers' note Use this sheet in conjunction with page 56, What's the time, Mr Wolf?, or as a stand alone activity to practise reading the time on an analogue clock face. The worksheet could also be copied onto card and laminated to create a more permanent resource.

**100% New Developing Mathematics
Understanding Shapes and
Measures: Ages 7–8
© A & C BLACK**

57

TV times: 1

- **Cut out these cards, and the cards from TV times: 2.**
- **Sort them into pairs.**

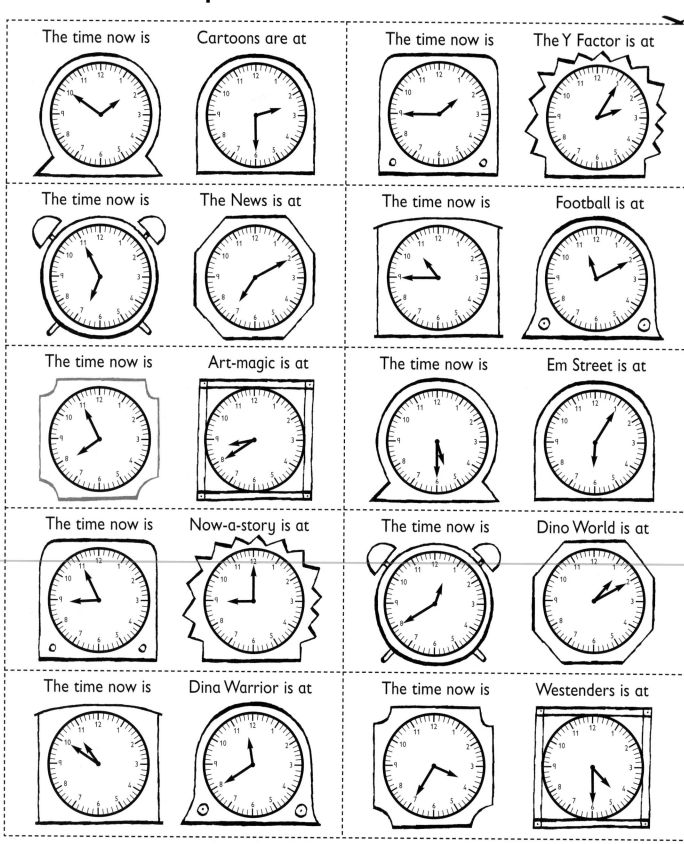

The time now is	Cartoons are at	The time now is	The Y Factor is at
The time now is	The News is at	The time now is	Football is at
The time now is	Art-magic is at	The time now is	Em Street is at
The time now is	Now-a-story is at	The time now is	Dino World is at
The time now is	Dina Warrior is at	The time now is	Westenders is at

Teachers' note Use this sheet in conjunction with page 59, TV times: 2. The children could also be given this sheet only and asked to write how long they would have to wait for each programme to start. Both sets of cards could also be used by children working in pairs, to play games such as Pairs, Snap or Pelmanism.

**100% New Developing Mathematics
Understanding Shapes and
Measures: Ages 7–8
© A & C BLACK**

TV times: 2

- **Cut out these cards, and the cards from TV times: 1.**
- **Sort them into pairs.**

I must wait for **25** minutes.

I must wait for **50** minutes.

I must wait for **45** minutes.

I must wait for **40** minutes.

I must wait for **15** minutes.

I must wait for **35** minutes.

I must wait for **20** minutes.

I must wait for **55** minutes.

I must wait for **5** minutes.

I must wait for **30** minutes.

Teachers' note Use this sheet in conjunction with page 58, TV times: 1. The children could also be given this sheet only and a set time, and asked to write at what time each programme would start. Both sets of cards could also be used by children working in pairs to play games such as Pairs, Snap or Pelmanism.

100% New Developing Mathematics Understanding Shapes and Measures: Ages 7–8 © A & C BLACK

Time interval loop cards

What time
would it be
2 hours later?

What time
would it be
10 minutes later?

What time
would it be
$\frac{1}{2}$ an hour earlier?

What time
would it be
5 hours later?

What time
would it be $\frac{3}{4}$ of
an hour earlier?

What time
would it be
10 minutes later?

What time
would it be
2 hours earlier?

What time
would it be
50 minutes later?

What time would
it be 40 minutes
earlier?

What time
would it be
6 hours later?

What time would
it be $\frac{1}{4}$ of an
hour earlier?

What time
would it be
5 minutes later?

What time would
it be 45 minutes
earlier?

What time
would it be
4 hours later?

What time
would it be
40 minutes later?

What time
would it be
2 hours earlier?

Teachers' note Give a loop card to each child in a large group (two sets could be used to make 32 cards). Choose a child to say the time and read the question. The first child to stand up with the correct card reads out the time and the new question. Alternatively, the cards can be used as an individual or pair activity where the children place them correctly in a loop.

100% New Developing Mathematics Understanding Shapes and Measures: Ages 7–8 © A & C BLACK

At the airport

• **Write how long it is before each plane leaves.**

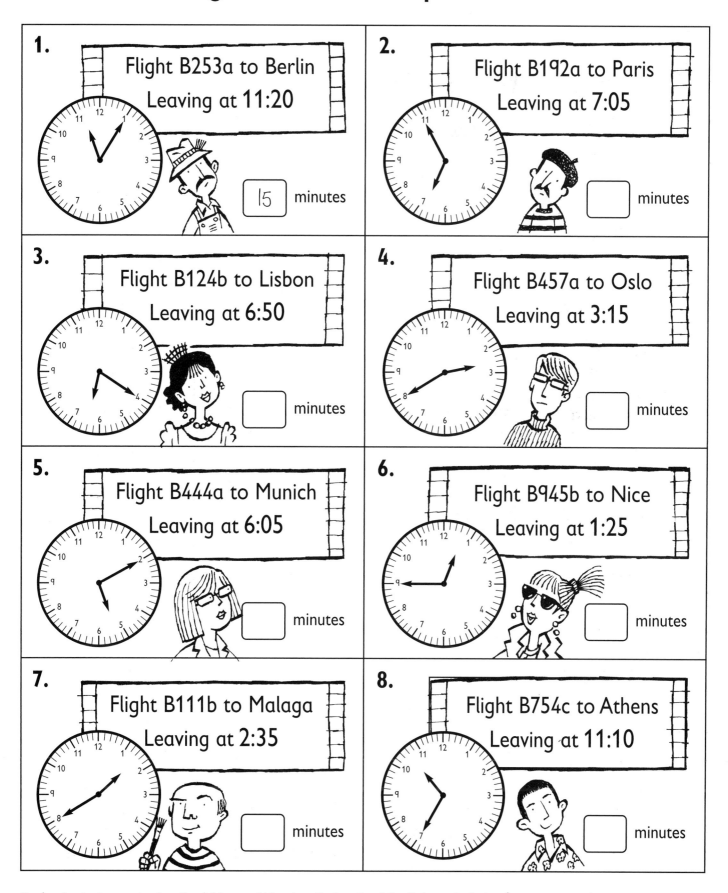

1.
Flight B253a to Berlin
Leaving at **11:20**

[15] minutes

2.
Flight B192a to Paris
Leaving at **7:05**

[ ] minutes

3.
Flight B124b to Lisbon
Leaving at **6:50**

[ ] minutes

4.
Flight B457a to Oslo
Leaving at **3:15**

[ ] minutes

5.
Flight B444a to Munich
Leaving at **6:05**

[ ] minutes

6.
Flight B945b to Nice
Leaving at **1:25**

[ ] minutes

7.
Flight B111b to Malaga
Leaving at **2:35**

[ ] minutes

8.
Flight B754c to Athens
Leaving at **11:10**

[ ] minutes

Teachers' note As an extension, the children could be given the lengths of the flights and asked to work out the arrival times in each of the destinations, for example the Nice flight is 2 hours and 20 minutes, the Athens flight is 3 hours 10 minutes, etc.

**100% New Developing Mathematics
Understanding Shapes and
Measures: Ages 7–8
© A & C BLACK**

- ## Play this game with a partner.

You need one counter and a dice.

☆ Start by placing the counter anywhere on the trail.

☆ Take turns to roll the dice and move the counter forward.

☆ Answer the question and cross off the time on your time strip.

☆ Cross off five times in a row on your strip to win the game.

A TV show starts at 3:30. It lasts for three-quarters of an hour. What time does it end?	Half an hour ago, a TV show started at 3:55. What time is it now?	A TV show has been on for quarter of an hour. The time now is 5:10. What time did it start?
A TV show starts at quarter to four. It lasts for one hour. What time does it end?		A film lasts for $1\frac{1}{2}$ hours. It will end at twenty past six. What time did it start?
A film finishes at five past six. If it has been on for 2 hours, what time did it start?		A TV show finishes at five past five. If it has been on for 25 minutes, what time did it start?
A quarter of an hour ago, a TV show started at five to four. What time is it now?		Three-quarters of an hour ago, a TV show started at 3:35. What time is it now?
A TV show has been on for three-quarters of an hour. It is now 5.20. What time did it start?		A film lasts for $1\frac{1}{4}$ hours. It began at 3:15. What time does it end?
A TV show starts at twenty to four. It lasts for 45 minutes. What time does it end?	A TV show finishes at half past five. It has been on for 55 minutes. What time did it start?	A TV show starts at quarter past three. It lasts for 45 minutes. What time does it end?

Player 1's time strip

4:00	4:05	4:10	4:15	4:20	4:25	4:30	4:35	4:40	4:45	4:50	4:55

Player 2's time strip

4:00	4:05	4:10	4:15	4:20	4:25	4:30	4:35	4:40	4:45	4:50	4:55

Teachers' note The children should move the counter in a clockwise direction.

100% New Developing Mathematics Understanding Shapes and Measures: Ages 7–8
© A & C BLACK

Answers

p 14
Possible answers:
1. triangle
2. (a) 4 **(b)** quadrilateral (rhombus)
3. (a) 4 **(b)** quadrilateral (trapezium)
4. (a) 3, 4 or 6 **(b)** triangle, quadrilateral (parallelogram) or hexagon
5. (a) 4, 5, 6 or 7 **(b)** quadrilateral (trapezium), pentagon, hexagon, heptagon

p 15
One possible solution:

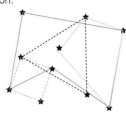

p 17
1. 3 **2.** 4 **3.** 4 **4.** 4 **5.** 4 **6.** 4 **7.** 4 **8.** 4

Now try this!
The shapes in questions 3, 4 and 5 are the same.
The shapes in questions 6 and 8 are the same.

p 18
1. red: square-based pyramid orange: triangular prism green: cylinder
2. red: cone orange: cube green: triangular prism
3. red: cylinder orange: cone green: sphere

p 19

	At least one circular face	No circular faces
At least one vertex	cone	cube cuboid prism (triangular) pyramid (square-based)
No vertices	cylinder	sphere

Now try this!

	At least one rectangular face	No rectangular faces
Prism	cube cuboid cylinder prism (triangular)	
Not a prism	pyramid (square-based)	cone sphere

p 21
✓ ✓ ✗ ✓ ✗
✓ ✓ ✓ ✗ ✓
✗ ✓ ✓ ✓ ✓

Now try this!
Line 2 shape 3 should be coloured green.
Line 3 shape 5 should be coloured blue.
Line 1 shape 1 should be coloured yellow.

p 22
Now try this!
1. square **2.** square= **3.** rectangle **4.** triangle **5.** hexagon
6. octagon **7.** quadrilateral (kite)

p 23

1.   **2.**

3. 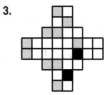 **4.**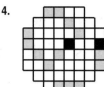

5. 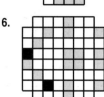 **6.**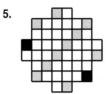

p 25

p 28
1. N3, E7, S1, W6, S1, E6, S1, W6
2. N1, E2, S1, E1, N2, W3, N1, E4, S3, E1, N1, E1, S1, E1, N2, W2, N1, E2
3. N3, E1, S1, E1, N1, E1, S2, W2, S1, E6, N1, W3, N2, E1, S1, E1, N1, E1, S1
4. N1, E1, S1, E6, N3, W1, S2, W4, N1, W2, N1, E5, S1, W2

p 29
1. F7 **2.** D2 **3.** F7 **4.** A3 **5.** B5

p 30
1. 8 cm East **2.** 12 cm West
3. $2\frac{1}{2}$ cm South **4.** 4 cm North
5. $3\frac{1}{2}$ cm South **6.** 10 cm West

63

p 32

1.

2.

3.

4.

p 33

Less than	Right angle	More than
AM	AN	AS
GO	ME	HE
BE	IS	TO
ON	BY	IT
MY	AT	
IN	OH	
HI		
SO		

p 36

1. 400   **2.** 700   **3.** 200   **4.** 300
5. 100   **6.** 50   **7.** 10   **8.** 650
9. 2500   **10.** 1000   **11.** 25   **12.** 75

Now try this!

(a) 5 m 18 cm   **(b)** 9 m 0 cm
(c) 1 m 50 cm   **(d)** 3 m 50 cm
(e) 1 m 25 cm   **(f)** 3 m 75 cm
(g) 1 m 20 cm   **(h)** 0 m 75 cm

p 37

1. 50   **2.** 30   **3.** 95
4. 83   **5.** 76   **6.** 33
7. 72   **8.** 65   **9.** 41

Now try this!
(a) 152   **(b)** 46

p 38

1. true   **2.** false   **3.** true
4. true   **5.** true   **6.** true

Now try this!
Caz lives about 2000 m from school.
Ella lives about 1500 m from school.

p 39
Questions 1, 3, 4, 5, 7, 8, 10, 11 and 12 should be coloured.

p 40
1. second child   **2.** first child
3. first child   **4.** first child
5. second child   **6.** second child

Now try this!
(a) second child   **(b)** first child

p 43
1. 14 cm   **2.** 12$\frac{1}{2}$ cm   **3.** 22 cm
4. 40 cm   **5.** 29 cm

p 45
No. (Total is about xx cm to the nearest half-centimetre and xx cm to the nearest tenth of a centimetre.)

p 46
1. 100 g   **2.** 30 m   **3.** 300 l   **4.** 25 cm
5. 500 g   **6.** 400 ml   **7.** 40 cm   **8.** 70 cm

p 47
1. 17 cm   **2.** 25 cm   **3.** 12 cm
4. 29 cm   **5.** 21 cm   **6.** 26 cm

p 48
Now try this!

1. 54 minutes   **2.** 15 minutes   **3.** 39 minutes
4. 23 minute   **5.** 2 minutes   **6.** 37 minutes
7. 43 minutes   **8.** 6 minutes   **9.** 21 minutes

p 50
Now try this!

400 ml	950 ml	750 ml
450 ml	350 ml	925 ml
975 ml	825 ml	575 ml

p 52-53
BEING CHEERFUL KEEPS YOU HEALTHY

p 55
1. 1:50   **2.** 5:10   **3.** 3:45   **4.** 8:40
5. 7:15   **6.** 2:35   **7.** 10:50   **8.** 9:25

p 58-59
40 mins = Cartoons
20 mins = Y Factor
15 mins = The News
25 mins = Football
45 mins = Art-magic
35 mins = Em Street
5 mins = Now-a-story
30 mins = Dino World
50 mins = Dina Warrior
55 mins = Westenders

p 61
1. 15   **2.** 10   **3.** 30   **4.** 35
5. 55   **6.** 40   **7.** 55   **8.** 35